Ascendance

Profound Spiritual Wisdoms

*Open to any page for contemplation, insights,
encouragement, and guidance.*

Nancy Clark, Ph.D

From the author of *Our Divinity Revealed*
and *Master Plant Teachers*

KNOW THYSELF AS DIVINITY

© 2023 Nancy Clark

All rights reserved. No part of this book may be reproduced or transmitted in any form or by any means without written permission of the publisher, except in the case of brief quotations embedded in critical articles, books, and reviews.

This material has been written and published solely for educational purposes. The author and the publisher shall have neither liability nor responsibility to any person or entity with respect to any loss, damage, or injury caused or alleged to be caused directly or indirectly by the information contained in this book.

The intent of the author is only to offer information of a general nature to help the reader in the quest for well-being. In the event the reader uses any of the information in this book of self or others, which is a constitutional right. The author and the publisher assume no responsibility for the actions of the reader.

Statements made and opinion expressed in this publication are those of the author and do not necessarily reflect the views of the publisher or indicate an endorsement by the publisher.

Published by

Dr. Nancy Clark, Ph.D. Publishing | nancyclarkphd.com

Publisher's Cataloging-in-Publication Data
Clark, Nancy.

Ascendance : profound spiritual wisdoms / Nancy Clark. – Flagler Beach, FL : Nancy Clark, PH.D. Pub., 2023.

p. ; cm.

ISBN13: 978-0-9601187-8-6 (softcover)
978-0-9601187-9-3 (hardcover)

1. Spirituality. 2. Spiritual life. I. Title.

BL624.C53 2023
204.4--dc23

Project coordination by Jenkins Group, Inc. | www.jenkinsgroupinc.com

Printed in the United States of America

27 26 25 24 23 • 5 4 3 2 1

*To Divine Source, who goes by thousands of names.
The pathway to you is love.
You dance to the delight in many forms.
Creation is unique expressions of you.
Your Divine Essence is hidden within,
but wise are those who recognize you.
O Beloved, the recognition of Source within
are those who are lost in your love.
We are together everywhere, like the wave and the ocean.*

Contents

Acknowledgments
vii

Ascendance
1

Profound Spiritual Wisdoms
3

Enchantment
167

Precious One
168

Beloved's Arrow
169

A Mystical Journey
171

About the Author
173

Acknowledgments

I would like to thank Divine Source for this unique expression of life and the ability to serve the Divine Plan. I would like to express my gratitude to all the people who have come into my life who have reminded me of my true identity, without whom this book would not have been possible—so many teachers who all had something to add and cause the remembrance, including the Master Plant Teacher, Mother Ayahuasca. I want to honor so many beautiful souls who have walked along with me, some for a short while and others for much longer. I applaud you, brave souls, for coming into this world to understand more deeply your true identity as a piece of Source by experiencing the illusion of separation.

Ascendance

Dancing with the Beloved is sweet Ascendance
Divine Infinite Love is seen Within All
Disguising Itself Within All creation
Break your connection with your false identity
See only my face as you walk through life

My lantern Within shines brightly
You are so precious to me
Worth more than all the fortunes
You are me in disguise experiencing this frolic
I listen for what delights your Soul

Direct mystical experience provides wisdoms of
the non-existence, ecstasy, purification
Love provides the glasses to see the invisible
Contemplate beyond the Human Temple body, look deeper Within
You are like a new lover, I created your beauty

I look to capture your attention
Uncover your outer reality, saturate you in my Love
Ascendance is like a slow dance together
I wait patiently for you, my lover to come to me
My dear lover, completely give in, to the beloved

—Nancy Clark

Ascendence began before incarnating into this physical life. This earthly life prepares one for the spiritual attainments. When a person is ready, the desire to enjoy the bliss of Oneness with the Divine comes. A higher reality is reached where the person stays with the Divine Presence. To stay in this higher reality requires absolute love and complete surrender.

Soul comes to know that true happiness comes from the Light and Sound attributes of Source. The daily spiritual practice is the connection and remembrance of this union with the Infinite.

The spiritual journey on earth begins with learning duality and all the lessons from life experiences. The pain and suffering, the joy and laughter, they are the mastery of duality. You have always been a Soul on an Infinite journey. In the beginning, you are consumed with the physical life. As the spiritual student advances in consciousness, these life experiences are the launch pad allowing the inner wisdoms, causing the courage and fortitude toward advancement.

Soul is the Doer, and when the spiritual student realizes their true identity through direct mystical experience of their Divine nature, they have graduated from the lower dimensions. If a

Master Soul desires to come back down to the lower planes, it is service to the Divine Plan.

When one feels loved, is it a fleeting moment? Or does it extend into all areas of their life and beyond? This deep compassion for oneself and all of life on this planet takes up a permanent residency.

Acceptance of the Divine Order is essential. Stay with the Higher Self perspective. The mind is the one that complains. The Soul sees perfection. The Higher Self has brought this to you to see your reaction, to polish you, to teach you. Continue on with acceptance.

True spirituality is portable. You should be able to take it wherever you go. The spiritual path is within you. You come to know you are the path. You and the spiritual path are One. This Oneness pervades throughout the universe.

When difficulties come up, stay in inner communication with your Higher Self. Then the answer will come and/or the outer life will show a solution. It is best to stay connected as you go through your day.

True liberation is being able to move one's consciousness outside of the chattering mind. True liberation is also being able to move beyond the physical world.

Dual Reality (duality) is what your two eyes can see. Move to your heart chakra and be with Source.

The Highest Truth is an inward gaze. You have a right to be happy and stay with Source, your Higher Self. Let the Soul take you up. All you have to do is stay with this inner Presence.

Do not lose hope, for Source is always with you and is your Higher Self. Go inward and converse with your Soul.

See the Life Force in all things. Look deeper at all of life and have the awareness of Source disguised within.

Love the Divine more than anything else. Keep your connection and stay focused on this inner Divine Essence. Release desires, except only wanting to be with Source. Turning your face away from the world means you have surrendered your ego. Do not get lost in the world; stay with Source.

The promise of immortality is the birthright of the Soul.

Be the Master Soul. Be the Love. Source is watching inwardly. The Omnipresence and all-pervading power are living within all that is seen and unseen.

The Soul's journey consists of overcoming the lower dimensions of physical, emotional, and mental levels to be able to experience the glorious realms of Oneness. The highest Truth is beyond the dimensions of relative truth, which is duality. Absolute Truth is beyond all of the dream states of Source. The level of Source is Absolute Truth.

Purity is raising the consciousness from the physical world to the higher spiritual dimensions beyond the world of matter, time, and space. A consciousness that has awareness beyond space will not require movement of the body to experience objects on the other side of the room, planet, or galaxy. A consciousness sitting on the couch will not need to move the body in order to touch the flowers located on the table. Pure Awareness realizes it is within all, seen and unseen.

You are being guided, and the path will bring many options with variables. Choose the highest path, for you are never limited. Take a deep breath and go within. Feel the peace and silence as you connect with your Soul. You are the love of Source. You can experience this love at any moment when your attention connects with your heart. Source is present everywhere and within all.

Nothing is wasted, and all events are used by your Soul as deep wisdoms. Change and transition are benefits to your Soul. The expanded consciousness of your Soul remembers all the created identities and your origin.

Compassion heals you.

Soul requires the experience of physicality to experience all the potentialities during a life filled with challenges. Soul needs to master duality and therefore requires incarnating into a physical form. Care for your physical body, which is the temple of the Soul, by providing proper food, movement, and rest. You will one day wake up from this Waking Dream called Life. Learn to connect with Source to offer a greater outcome for yourself and humanity.

With the gift of Free Will, Souls choose to play in the Light or Darkness. Souls were created with the highest frequency of love. Beings who chose Light view life in Oneness and have compassion for all of creation. Beings who chose Darkness desire to deceive, and this turns to evil, causing more movement away from Source. Souls choose to work for the Divine Plan or have rebelled against the Divine Plan of Source. Light always prevails over Darkness regardless of appearances in the lower regions. Those who are harmed physically are covered in Light and return to their origin dimension. Shine your Light and remember your true identity as a piece of Source.

You have free will, and peace is a choice. Smile within as you feel the love that is all around you that is unseen. Transcend this reality by connecting to higher dimensions within. The moment you awaken to these other realities, you come to remember that you are a multidimensional being filled with many dimensions and densities.

Challenges in the form of problems will come. Do everything you can to resolve them as best you can, then release them to your Higher Self and ask for the best possible outcome for everyone involved. Once released, then surrender your attention to the problem and say, "Thy Will Be Done."

Keep your focus on the Highest Power. Your Soul can stay talking with Source all day regardless of what is going on in the world. As you go through your day, keep practicing the Presence and remembering your deep connection with Source.

Each morning, wake up and remember you are a Soul on an assignment here on Earth. You are on a mission for service to the Divine Plan. Keep the awareness that you are not from here. You are a foreigner in a foreign land and just a temporary visitor.

Detachment brings freedom from all physical, emotional, and mental states. Observation of real from unreal produces detachment.

When the student feels the effects of the magnificent Sound Current going through their beingness, deep-seated grooves of set behavioral patterns are transformed into spiritual wisdoms. The "Word" that the Bible talks about is the powerful Sound Current of Source that flows, continuously showering love that heals and brings gratitude for being a unique expression and experiences peace that surpasses all understanding of the conscious mind. After this mystical experience, the spiritual student knows this transformation is now a reality.

Spiritual practices offer experience with the Divine. The conscious mind cannot take you to dimensions above the mental region. Dining with Truth provides the fruits so easily revealed to the practicing spiritual student that the intellectuals are frustrated with only the topics and not the true essence of the arcane mysteries.

Duality is a catalyst for evolution. Remember your Divine Origin. You are in the Cosmic University.

We are all extensions of Source experiencing creation, Divinity of Source manifesting in unique expressions.

Angelic beings, spirit guides, and the Higher Self are with the seeker, continuously waiting for acknowledgment. Once recognition occurs, that help is always there; the person can reach out requesting guidance and help at any moment. This energy as focused attention transports the spiritual student to these higher dimensions instantly. The student's team of helpers are quickly on the requested project. Ideas, realizations, downloads, and external situations are experienced by the seeker, which verifies that help is there working on their behalf.

Until the person comes to the realization that this is a Waking Dream, everything in this life will have power over them. If they get lost in the dream, they just reawaken and remember that they are living out experiences in a lower reality. It is just a dream; it's not the highest reality of Source. Their first mistake was taking it to be real.

When Soul awareness has been awakened, balance in both worlds is visible in the spiritual student's life. The spiritual life leads the physical life.

The illusions of this world cause a covering over the inner third eye. True awakened consciousness opens up the mysteries of spirit.

The seeker is to surrender completely to the Most Powerful Force of Existence. What the spiritual student is being led to do can be trusted when asked from the Living Essence that created all of life. When possible, they contemplate on how much of their selves are greatly loved, and they rely on this Infinite Presence Within. As the person gets used to remembering, a wonderful serenity comes with flawless vision that enters immediately.

Ascension of consciousness comes by way of many steps. Soul Energy needs to be preserved and utilized for the spiritual journey. As a person advances, the viewpoint will transform with luminousness transparency, insights, and enthusiasm to serve the Divine Plan.

The true enemies are those who try to divide us and humanity. When you have connected with your individuality, you have broken your connection with the universe.

Do you spend more time in your mind or with your Higher Self? Watch and observe the mental chatter. Let those thoughts go. Watch the thoughts. See the future version of you now.

Learn to chuckle, because you see through the Matrix while you stand in it. Learn to be the Observer. When someone starts to yell, walk away, because you are in control. Play the game and move through life with no anger and no resentment. Don't let them control you by getting angry. Recognize you are in the Matrix. Step into what you want to be doing. Being the Observer is what helps navigate this game of life.

Life Review is when you feel how the person you hurt felt. You experience the hurt you imposed upon them.

The only thing that separates us from the Divine is our misguided perception. You are a sacred Soul of Infinite Light.

Thoughts are more destructive to the body because it is energy. Watch the thoughts. The body can process food easier than negative energy.

Watch yourself playing in duality. It is just part of the human experience. Stay in Neutrality. Watch yourself moving out of judging. Duality is always a choice. Don't play in Duality. Stand in Duality, yet do not play in it. Be the Observer. Don't judge Duality, just accept it.

Give them Love. Give them Compassion. Laughter creates Joy. People will be attracted to you. Be in Balance.

Detachment is huge! It releases suffering. Stay in a place of nonjudgment. What is happening is for you, not to you. Everything is working in your favor regardless of appearances. Be okay with pain. Life did not promise an easy ride. How much greater are you by going through this experience?

This Fear has Nothing on you! Let go of all fear. We are truly blessed.

Your words hold a frequency. Your thoughts hold a frequency. Your emotions hold a frequency. Your actions hold a frequency. Food and water hold frequencies. Choose wisely.

Don't search externally for happiness and fulfillment. Stay present and you will receive a lot more spiritual download.

At any moment we can go back and remember what we saw during an inward mystical experience. We are all lost until we find Home. We can visit it from time to time. When we translate, we can experience Home since we are out of this dimension. We came here to help those who got lost along the journey. We came here to help others wake up. We knew what we were up against. The Fog, the Adversary, and the Veil wipe our memory.

You are blessed with Source Light. Shine your light onward and upward.

How you treat others is important. Try not to get upset. You need to laugh more. Enjoy your life, self-care, time outdoors. Close your eyes at any moment and you will find peace.

Have compassion for others, for they are asleep and don't know they are programmed.

You are here to be of service.

Fear is expensive. Love is real. Choose wisely.

You think you came here to not be in the dark? You are a Lightworker. Your light dissolves the shadow.

Work on yourself first! Your greatest resource is yourself. It is called Divine Intelligence. Love yourself throughout this life. More compassion, more love. Watch the thoughts.

People ask, "Why doesn't God do something?" Source has done something, and that was established at our creation. Free Will allows for us to create and grow our life garden. How we care for our own gardens determines how beautifully they spread out. We are forced to work at our deliverance in this era of space and time. It is a blessing to be given the wisdom on how to do so. Remain anchored to Source Frequency.

Change for the better by raising the frequency of the world. Be a transmitter of peace, trust, and well-being. Shining your light for this world transforms the vibrations and anchors the light.

Observe your moments. Be the Observer. Are you in your head? Or are you in your Higher Self?

The basic building blocks of this reality are protons, neutrons, and electrons. Quantum electrodynamics shows a deeper part of reality where the Light interacts with time and space. The atom is the smallest unit that holds consciousness. This has been proven by scientists. Experiments showed how the atoms behaved differently when they were being watched by the scientists' consciousness. A consciousness recognizes when another consciousness is observing, and interaction occurs.

Be Love. How are you choosing to Be in this moment? How are you Being? Visualize Love blanketing the planet. The frequency of Love is what you are.

We are all One. Be at peace and be in the Light.

There was an ancient king who had a dream of being a butterfly. He questioned this reality by asking, "Am I a king having a dream of being a butterfly? Or am I a butterfly having a dream of being a king?" Don't be fooled by the appearances of this world and therefore take it to be real. It is the Waking Dream.

A person is already complete. It is the mind that feels incomplete and therefore takes from someone else to feel they are getting ahead. Soul, being the Divine Essence, is already complete. The Soul watches and observes the antics of the mind. Know Thyself as Divinity places your attention on the actions of your mind. The Soul needs to be the one in control of the mind. The traps and illusions of "more is better" are from the mind. We want to be noticed by our essence.

Constant action is an addiction. There needs to be time spent connecting with your Divine Essence, your Higher Self, the Soul. There will come a day on your spiritual journey when you will need to simplify your life. This will rest your mind because you realize it has become so chaotic, agitated, angry, upset, depressed, and unhappy. You will realize the value of creating a more peaceful environment.

Higher Light Hierarchs and Cocreators are constantly watching and help us while we are in service while on our assignments on Earth.

The spontaneous tears are part of the mystical journey. Do not be alarmed; this is the Soul being saturated with Divine Love. The Soul is raptured with this deep connection with Source. There is no sobbing, for the tears just flow quietly and uncontrolled, and an inward gaze comes over the person. These are profound moments, and what is stated internally is "Thy Will Be Done." Another internal vow is "I will do my best to serve the Divine Plan."

If you get lost in the physical reality, listen to your breath. Feel the breath come in and then go out. This is the Life Force coming in, and then the next breath brings another connection with Source.

When we connect to our Higher Self, this is a vacation from our mind. We are above the lower dimensions of time, space, and matter and emotional and mental regions. The Soul is always there, yet we are unable to hear and connect with this internal compass unless we are able to go beyond the constantly chattering mind.

A spiritual student on a mystical journey who has been on this path for a while may experience a plateau. The person has reached a higher-vibrational level of consciousness and has no support, for others around them are working on mastering the initial stages. This student needs to be with higher-level spiritual students working on spiritual mastership or who have moved to an even higher level. Master Soul Teachers are needed, for they have moved through these levels and can work with the students showing by example. A master-level teacher helps by offering spiritual discussions and guidance, teaching the mastery of the wisdoms, and at some point creating a spiritual community. The spiritual classes, retreats, and community events help with evolutionary growth, awakening, integration, and spiritual mastership. A spiritual community is a resource for the spiritual student. They help each other when a fellow member in the community gets caught by the world.

The remembrance of your True Identity is only the first step, yet it is vital on the mystical journey. When the student has gone beyond the duality of love and hate, everything is seen with clarity and nothing is hidden. As long as the student identifies with anything other than their Divinity, they will see everything as separate and not in a state of Oneness. Don't try to walk away from your human life in order to get to your Divinity. Also, don't focus on Divinity and neglect your human life. While you are in physical form, you are experiencing the lessons.

Seek a spiritual teacher who will teach in person. The internet is a great resource, yet my spiritual master teachers taught me in person. Videos and online classes are helpful, yet the integration into daily life is the mastery. For a person making this transition without a spiritual community, it is extremely difficult. When the spiritual student levels out, then what do they do? To become a spiritual master in their own right takes a teacher who will want to see them reach spiritual mastery at all levels. Once spiritual mastership is reached, the teacher is quick to release them and enjoys seeing them walking the Earth at this achieved level. A master-level teacher produces a spiritual master. Master-level students are encouraged to go on to teach by example the spiritual principles and the mystical journey and to get their students to reach the high spiritual attainments of Self-Realization and

God Realization. The master teacher knows their time on this planet is temporary and creates replacements that will go on to teach Souls ready for these spiritual attainments long after their teacher has left the planet. This is the legacy of love.

Every day surrender your ego to Source.

Spiritual freedom is attainment of mastership. Freedom from the illusion of the physical, emotional, and mental planes for these levels is temporary. The higher dimensions are beyond time, space, matter, physical body, emotional body, and mental body. Freedom from all of these coverings over the Soul is true freedom.

When a seeker sends out a sincere request to the Divine Essence to reach a higher spiritual level, a verification is experienced to their loving petition. The student sees the manifestation of their next spiritual teacher. There is a heartfelt call that goes out, and the universe responds lovingly to any Soul who wants to reunite with Source.

Some spiritual students will need instruction to go, to fly, to get up there into the upper dimensions. Other students will already be up there and so far out that they will need instruction on how to ground themselves and live on this planet. The dance begins by balancing the Divine Life and the Physical Life.

Pain and suffering are due to the illusion of separateness. A sense of unity comes from the truth that we are all a part of the One Infinite Essence that permeates All and IS All. When we see despair in our culture, this means humanity is ready for the mystical journey. The sadness, greed, fear, and unhappiness are opportunities for moving to the next level and the willingness to search for meaning in life. Many times, a situation will cause a person to look at their life and ask for meaning.

The Absolute Powerful Source knew Itself before creation. This Infinite Frequency began to create out of nothingness. The Ethers are filled with the Glorious Awareness. The Primordial Sound explodes into the void of timelessness, causing the Light to manifest. A wave expanded and grew, generating outbursts with expressions of Itself, producing heat with extreme power that created suns, the pieces of which would become stars. Expansion grew, bringing forth multiverses. Source Love Frequency desired to experience Itself throughout infinity. Many Souls were created with the expression of Elohim. Their boundlessness manifestation is of the Divine Source. The Elohim is beyond name or form. Eternity would call these Souls the Elohim. They knew themselves as ONE. Other Souls that were created later would refer to them as the Elohim. They are the Divine Essence of Source that only identifies themselves with their foreverness having the power of the ONE. The Soul group called the Elohim would later create bodies as a gift from the Everlasting Spirit. Their destiny caused them to know Light and Darkness. All Souls at some point undergo life in the lower dimensions to comprehend their own creative power, true Divine nature, and unique individual expressivity with the Oneness of Source.

An awakened Soul can separate Truth from illusion.

The word "karma" itself simply means "action." These actions are ill-thought-out decisions or wise decisions, otherwise known as the Law of Cause and Effect. It feels disciplining until the student complies with the spiritual evolutionary system. One of the steps to spiritual mastery is having control over all decisions and thus mastering this spiritual law.

True spiritual surrender induces intentional, voluntary choice in service to whatever is asked of oneself.

As a person travels the spiritual path, dilemmas can take on a new meaning. A change in the path's direction causes one to face new opportunities, challenges, and people. Allow the solution to take form and it will manifest into the physical and mental areas of life.

Your view of your successes and failures will decide your liberty from the physical plane.

You have been informed of the upcoming spiritual journey. The seeker becomes the student. Divine law instruction comes when the seeker sends out an internal request for the highest-vibrational teacher to come into their life.

The mind only hears the utterance of verbalism, whereas the Soul has transparency through the fulfilment of it.

You are so blessed to be able to reside in the Divine Presence. Source is calling you back Home; awaken to your Divinity. At any moment you can relax and connect with Source, for that is your true nature, your birthright, and your heritage.

When you consent to this physical reality as being true, it has power over you.

When the need arises, call on the Higher Self's love and guidance for all areas of your life.

The unfoldment process allows Soul to emerge and start taking the prominent role instead of the ego.

At a certain evolutionary level, discipline is not required, for resistance is absent because the identification with Source is present. An advanced Soul loves all because of the realization that Source is Within All.

Who are you really? Source disguised as a human. Your true nature is Divinity, and Source lives within you.

The Divine holds you as a delicate flower, safeguarding your unfoldment in daily life.

Advanced spiritual teachers do not require perfection or a moral code of their students; rather, they teach that spiritual mastery is the desired state. Control at all levels of physical, emotional, and mental affairs is apparent in their daily life.

Your greatest lover is within you. All you have to do is turn inward and accept this eternal love of Beloved Source.

Depending upon the ego is in vain.

Master Soul teachers aim their arrows energetically for the awakened Souls. The advanced spiritual teacher is looking to teach Souls ready to become spiritual masters.

The Higher Self decides when the Soul will leave the body. The Higher Self is the "Observer" in all situations. Sometimes the Higher Self will create situations for a person to venture out into in search of deeper meaning in their life.

Utmost assignments of ethereal beings are commissioned from the higher worlds to help in the spiritual evolution of asking Souls. Each seeker is required to ask for spiritual help because of the Law of Noninterference. No being is allowed to dominate over a person's Free Will. Each person has the power of choice. Spiritual awakening occurs with the emergence of wisdom on how the spiritual system works.

The pearl is formed from a constant irritant inside the shell of the living organism. Let your aggravation, frustration, and annoyance create pearls of wisdom in your life.

Your love for all of creation is to teach yourself how to love yourself. Source is with you and is within all as the Oneness of Divinity. We are all ONE family of Divine Beings.

You can talk with the Divine all day long.

Once a Soul has been touched by the Divine, the desire to become absorbed in the melodies of the harmonic celestial symphony causes intense intoxication of pure love.

When a certain vibrational level is reached, the Higher Self will reveal Itself to the conscious mind, letting it be known that it is now on the ascendent. The Soul will calm the mind, causing the surrendering process to begin. The ego begins to become intoxicated with the melodies of the Divine Symphony. Soul moves toward service to the Divine Plan.

Each Soul has a unique wavelength called an Energetic Signature Frequency, for this is your spiritual fingerprint.

Direct mystical experience offers firsthand observation or participation of absolute truth transcending all mental knowledge.

The mind lives off of the Soul power, for it can't work with the sustaining energy of Source within. Divine Truth cannot be understood by the mind completely. At a certain level, the Soul needs to have direct personal experience, and then the mind cannot explain it away, for a new reality opens up. Self-Realization and God Realization are attainments that require direct mystical experience above the mental plane.

Be watchful of people who accuse others around them. This is a psychic attack caused by a negative ego being projected onto others around them by sending negative thoughts of false accusations. Some people let off steam by yelling at and venting to others around them. Spiritually protect yourself from negative attacks.

Always choose harmlessness toward others and live a spiritually principled lifestyle. Hold loving and neutral thoughts toward others, even those who have harmed you. Disconnect from hurtful people for self-preservation. Forgive from a safe distance and wish for their Soul growth as the Divine wills it to be.

The mind becomes scattered while handling duties in the outside world. Communion with the Divine requires bringing Soul's energy inward. Develop a time for spiritual connection where the mind can rest and the Soul can remember this Oneness with Pure Source Energy.

It is Divinely planned for you to be holding this book, for you are a Lightworker. If you are ever unsure about your purpose work, you came here to help in the raising of the collective consciousness on this planet. Your light and frequency were needed here on Earth.

The attainment of Mastership is achieved through adversity, discipline, and a longing for Oneness.

When residing at a higher vibration, your heart is open and works for the highest good for others. This is when you have reached the Wisdom of the Real Light. Know that you are on a journey toward Home. Humanity is one large family. Remember to dance in the Light.

It is not your responsibility to solve others' problems for them. You can offer options to them, yet the person has to make decisions for their own life. Each person has to take ownership and responsibility for their own life. Personal accountability is key in spiritual mastery.

Your power is your ability to remain neutral in a highly charged duality environment. Negative egos like to throw their harmful lower frequencies at your consciousness. An individual who is spiritually oriented and committed to living a harmonious life of balance with both spirit and the physical has protection. If you are struggling now, your spiritual function is to love yourself and get your mind under your Higher Self's direct control. Make an effort to stop allowing negative behaviors to impact you regardless of who is doing what.

You are a Soul in Action. Emotions will cause an ever-changing motion in perceptions. Stay connected with Source for the highest Truth and the clearest perception. A higher purpose is the Divine Plan. Free Will allows duality to exist. Many Souls harmonize with the Light, and many Souls align with Darkness.

The Higher Realms only know Absolute Truth and resonate in this Divine Essence. Remember who you are. Your power is in the Light. Find ways to promote peace. Love and Peace are Within. This is not your home. You came from magnificence and will return to splendor.

Who are you? You are Light. You are Power. You are Wisdom. In order to understand the meaning of everything, you had to become everything, by living everything. Reach for the promises of Light when others attack you with words. Remember that you are infinite. Love cannot be divided or denied but is eternal. Rest in this love.

Bathe in the Healing Love. You are coming into a state of Pure Awareness. This is your true state of being. There is no conflict when you reside in the Light. Find a place that provides peace and live there. Peace is priceless. You may have to sacrifice familiarity. Peace shows the power of love in action. Peace brings remembrance that you are so loved.

When you reside in the highest frequency of Love, you energetically draw people and circumstances to you for the best interest of all. Trust in the Sacred Essence, this Source Within All life. You carry this power Within. Find this truth within. Keep this evolved perspective that you are not alone. Share this and the

Light will spread. Many Souls need the Light that you carry. You are needed on this planet. Shine brightly in this dark world.

Workers of Light: We are infinitely connected to each other, as we carry the essence of Source Within. We are the collective of the Divine. Stay awake and aware. This path is one of greater power and purpose. At any moment you can breathe deep and find a place in peace. You are consciousness and therefore are infinite and sacred. Who is the one looking out of your eyes? You are not in this reality without help and assistance. You have friends in high places.

Transcend the identification with this lower world by experience through a Self-Realization state of consciousness.

Source Frequency is always instantly available. Connect with your Soul, who is a piece of the Omnipotent Source. You are a part of everything. Only in this Waking Dream do you feel alone and forsaken. You are One with Divine Source.

Source did not create evil races of beings. There is Free Will, and each Soul chooses to act in Light or Darkness. The Divine allows freedom of choice. You get to choose to love Supreme

Source back. The Beloved knows you and what you are feeling at this moment. Your hearts are One. If you have lost hope, other Souls are waiting to remind you of your majesty. Walk the spiritual path together. We live as One in the Light.

Soul advancement requires challenges and pain for the highest evolution. If you had no lessons, nothing would be learned. This human experience offers intense classes in the Cosmic University. Be strong and carry on; continue toward your degrees in the form of spiritual attainments. Your next assignment after this life is selected based on how well you passed your exams.

This is a glorious celebration when you return Home. As you complete this life story, your consciousness has full perception. This is only a Waking Dream, and you will continue on with other adventures. You will be greeted with joy and laughter by those who left the physical plane before you. The end will be your beginning. You have friends from many realms. Live your life as if it is a dream. Dreams allow you to create reality.

When you incarnated into physical form, you agreed to forget your origin. You entered the hologram, were programed, and believed what you were told. As you grew and became an adult, there was this feeling that you did not belong here. Move beyond the ego and align this Sacred Essence with your Higher Self.

You wanted to learn and understand by experiencing duality. You always have this Love and Light Within. You can access this at any moment.

Source emanates from you. You carry this power inside as you move through every moment. The higher perspective is to know you are this Light and are not alone. Connect with Light to overcome the Darkness that you see around you. Go to the place where peace resides within you. Your journey will have peaks and valleys. If a road ends, a new beginning awaits you. The Darkness may appear to be hindering the Light. The path is the journey to experience Darkness, duality, illusion; however, you are the Light that takes away the Darkness from the path. Persevere and conquer all Darkness with your Light.

Establish a heavenly link between the Infinite Creator and the Infinite Soul. You can experience the Kingdom of Heaven while inhabiting a human body.

The ego performs the Identity Theft. Ego: Edge God Out. Big ego provides large separation from one another. The ego has one desire: to be more powerful than the True Self. Soul gives awareness of True Identity as a piece of Source and unity consciousness. The chaos within us is the ego. We need to see the external chaos in order to see that we are capable of both Hate and Love. The Ego and Soul, Duality. You are to face your True Self and accept your True Identity. Wear your coat of awareness and watch the ego that is filled with anger, fear, greed, deception, and so on.

You are enough. Become silent and connect vibrationally to what is Real, the Sacred Source Frequency. Going within will bring strength to your beingness. Make decisions that will be beneficial to your Soul Life. Rise each morning with a knowingness and say, "I am on a Divine Assignment." You are a creative being, as you have learned to navigate through all your challenges in this life. Earth is your temporary home. You live in an environment of duality while you seek balance. Allow your True Essence to flow as you go along with your day. You are here by design and are filled with splendor. You are more powerful than you realize. Divine Presence experiences all your joys and struggles. Your path is the story of you.

The very life essence is Source Celestial Music, known by many names. This sustains all life seen and unseen in all the dimensions.

Pure freedom is the experience when a person has the awareness and power to move beyond the mind and choose the state of consciousness that draws them upward toward Divine Love.

Primordial Light becomes human eggs. Ovum egg is a perfect sphere. The Egg of Life is a sacred geometric pattern that creates all the living life forms. It forms bodies, right down to the eye color, and it created you. The geometric patterns relate to Light and Sound and tie it all together. The Egg of Life becomes the Flower of Life geometric pattern, then expands to be called the Fruit of Life. Atoms are the shape of a sphere. Light waves that move through space are all in the shape of spheres. Light is interactive spheres of atoms within the object. We have the periodic table of elements. Atoms create the molecules that make the fabric of reality. Geometry within the human body is organic chemistry.

You started out as a Supernova, for it is in your DNA, the same materials and star dust.

In the Hindu tradition there are five layers over the Soul:

> *Physical:* Anamaya Kosha
> *Energy:* Prana maya Kosha
> *Mental:* Mana maya Kosha
> *Wisdom:* Vijnana maya Kosha
> *Bliss:* Ananda maya Kosha

The Bliss provides the cosmic peace, beyond the mind. Be a Blissful Being and recognize our Oneness with All that is.

To be harmonious, you need to have a high vibration. Be in balance in what you Think, Feel, and Do. You can transform realities through Sound Vibration. The atoms sing with the Celestial Harmonic Symphony of Light and Sound that creates all the matter in this physical reality. You came down here to show how to live and become an enlightened being. Be an example of a highly evolved being. Show how to live properly in this third-dimensional reality that is a very low vibration.

Rainbow Body is the Light Body, being dissolved into Pure Light. Five Layers of Pure Light Energy:

    Soul / The I AM
    Etheric / Light Body
    Astral Body
    Mental Body
    Physical Body

You need to receive this awareness before leaving this world. Know of your perfection as a god, in physical form, having a human experience.

Permanent Awareness causes a person to live from the Soul state and be observant of the vibrations they are creating and living within. When a person has tasted the Divine ambrosia, it leaves an imprint for eternity. You are on an inner path. Somewhere along the way, the journey goes inward, causing a direct mystical experience that changes your viewpoint forever. Desire for the higher life leads you to spiritual liberation, causing ever-expanding consciousness throughout the process. Let your life be a walking Divine reflection.

Wheels are seen in Sacred Geometry. They are the keys to the harmonics of music/sound, keys to the dimensional harmonics. These wheels of dimensional levels are found on the ceilings in the Egyptian pyramids. These wheels are surrounded by stars carved into the ceilings of Egyptian temples.

Setting time aside for complete absorption frees them from the outer world of objects. The spiritual student should not run from the world but learn the values it teaches.

You are love. No force can prevail against you. You are Light from Source Light.

The celestial inner music is so enchanting that hearing it causes a person to start the spiritual quest. Many times, the person forgets about the physical world, for it becomes unreal, causing disinterest.

One fish said to another, "You are new here. How did you get to our river?" The other fish responded, "The ocean's strong current pushed me toward this river." The resident river fish asked, "What is the ocean like?" The ocean fish responded about all the magnificent qualities of the enormous ocean and then added, "If you are really interested in what it is like to swim in the ocean, I can take you there so you can experience it for yourself. There is nothing like swimming in the immense ocean."

In the beginning stage, the person needs to know what their true identity is, why they incarnated into the physical form, and what their purpose work is.

There are different levels of consciousness. To change the consciousness level, a person needs to modify the current vibration. All levels are a vibrational frequency, only as they move upward, it becomes more in harmony with Source.

It is not our ordinary daily duties that cause captivity but our mental attitudes toward our life's responsibilities. We can be happy doing the dishes while singing along to music or complaining about life.

The spiritual student's objective is to experience the Divine Source in their inner world. It is the Soul who has this union and realizations. The Soul experiences the pure bliss, highest truth, and deep contentment.

A Master Soul has the key that offers freedom from the ego. Only a wise person sees the value of the key that can free them from the prison cell of the ego.

The highest truth shows the spiritual student that they cannot be in bondage to the senses and have mastery over their world. To know the wisdom of truth, a person needs to acknowledge whether they are on the journey and whether they are in bondage.

Realize that there are two of you. The Lower Self AND the Higher Self. Lower Self ~ Ego, Mind, Personality. Higher Self ~ the Soul, the I AM, Spark of Source. The transformation is going from one identity to the other, identification from the Lower Self to the Higher Self. The person who came on this path does *not* exist, exists only in name. You need to discover that you are this other identity, the Soul. This is who you really are. Your energies are trapped in the body consciousness. You are a Soul. When you are still identifying with anything other than Soul, you are not going to be able to get beyond the physical dimension. The Seeker may ask, "How can I be different from what I know myself to be?" That is the adventure of the whole spiritual unfoldment. We want to know the eternal aspect of our own beingness, which is Soul. We want to live on the energy that inspires us. As we go along the spiritual journey, these cups of elixir are experienced as Love Waves. You start to realize there are two of you. There is your Spiritual Life, and then there is this Temporal Life. In time, you start to realize who you REALLY ARE. Your identity shifts, and you get to know your True Self. If you stay on the path of unfoldment for a long time, a new view comes; this is called Dual Consciousness. Who am I? Am I this mortal being? Or am I this Divine Being who feels this love and bliss from the Omnipotent Beloved who loves me and helps me in my life? Somewhere along the path, you get spiritual downloads. Those who take the time to connect to the Divine Presence receive more wisdoms. We must participate and try as best we can to stay close to the Beloved. Don't wander off too far.

Most people are hypnotized and unable to discern real from unreal. A student on a spiritual path will start to wake up and utilize this discernment power, and then discernment will increase. How does a person stay in this bliss in the Soul State? They start to discern what happens in their life. They no longer get flattened by what just comes in. When they start to feel anger toward someone in the past who hurt them, at that moment, they realize this and instead switch over and start to feel compassion, tolerance, and forgiveness, which are the remedies for anger. The spiritual student starts to realize there is a real contest going on here between the Lower Self and the Higher Self. What the Beloved is trying to get them to see is that they are the Higher Self. Truth is simple. You are a Soul, a Divine Being.

Everyone is paying devotion to something. What is special to you? A dog will look out the window for hours, waiting in devotion for their Beloved master, to be together again.

When you are in the Soul State, you are naturally drawn to the Divine Presence and cannot be without this connection, for it is automatic. Soul and the Divine Presence reside within the same area. When you transform yourself from the body consciousness to the Beloved, you will naturally resonate with the Divine Essence. You are connected, forever One. As you rise in spirituality, you will see the ego's antics and your Soul State. You will start to see more of your Lower Self. You will start to get all types of insights. Then in the Soul State, you remember that the Divine Presence is always with you. You really can contact that Love anytime you want. Now you are actually transcending your Lower Self. You want to know why your spiritual life is not better. You want to stay in the body consciousness. You want to hold on to things that have given you energy and distraction.

You get to a point where you say, "I want to be in the Soul State and live my life from the Higher Self perspective, only see myself as a Divine Being having a human journey." You must attain your Soul State every day and keep an eye on that Ego that likes to Edge God Out.

Selfless Service will take your energies and move them toward serving the Divine Plan. The higher you go, the more selfless service you will become. You will find that all you do is service. You have to live this path. These principles need to be applied to your life.

The Higher Self is impersonal and detached. The Lower Self takes things personally. The personal is the Ego. The impersonal is the Soul. The Ego makes everything a personal issue. The Soul is not going to get wrapped up in what the Ego says is real. Accept your own Soul-ness as your True Identity. When you get into your Soul-ness, then the Divine flows. You don't have to try at discipline, because you have it right at your fingertips. You don't want to be sitting down in your body with this Ego Identity all day. Stay in the Soul State of Being. You can't force this; it is a natural occurrence. Your love grows daily for the Divine Presence within. Surrender to it. Yes, you can strive for it. Yes, you can live your life the best you can and do your duties and disciplines. Stay in connection and it will happen. No matter what happens in your life, the physical world is just a virtual classroom. When you are in the Higher Self, you are in total harmony with the Divine. You have the power; you are the Soul. Upgrade your image of yourself. See yourself as a Divine Being.

At some point, you come to the Awake State. This state of consciousness offers release from the prison cell of the Lower Self. The Divine wants to come in and release you from your jail cell. You are starting to realize that there is a way you can live your life to make it a lot easier. This is the path of unfoldment. The Divine Presence is right with you. You will feel this vibration come in, and you will experience this Love. This is what fuels your desire to keep this connection and free yourself from the Lower Self. After a while, you are not going to want to be the slave to the senses, slave to your thoughts, with emotions out of control. When you get up higher, you start to see things more clearly. You may say, "I was a fool doing that, and now at a higher level I can understand my hurt, my pain, and why I had such a rough time." You see, we need this higher help.

Intense longing and separation are a reaction from being down here away from the Soul State, which is an aspect of the Divine Presence within you. Those are the pains of separation. Remember you are the Soul and Divine Presence. You must want to separate from your Lower Self, the Ego running your life. Those who are determined will get there. You will be able to manifest this Higher Self, the Soul State connection at any moment. When you are at the higher state of being, you will take hell and turn it into heaven. Stay connected to the Divine Presence and you can touch heaven and feel the Love come in instantaneously.

If you find people leaving your life, you no longer have to play out those situations anymore. The lessons have been learned or tests have received a higher grade. When your vibration has been raised, if the other person's frequency is lower, they will leave your life at some point. Sometimes we have to be the one to release them for self-preservation.

The path never ends. You never end. You will spend eternity in expansion. You never completely arrive. We all will spend eternity expanding and serving the Divine Plan. You don't want it to end. The adventures are endless.

Your body will become so sensitive that there will be foods you cannot eat.

Love transforms when you are amazed by your own spiritual beauty. Love purifies the Lower Self. Nothing is superior to Love. Get on the highway of Love. Eat it, drink it, bathe in it, and so forth. The love and peace will come when connecting with the Divine Presence. Approach all of life with balance. Balance is the key. Impose balance. Balance allows you to have all of life, and at the same time you can let it all go.

Consciousness has no form. It deals with awareness, truth, and the Soul, beyond the Lower Self, and it is always free. Consciousness is really who you are.

The spiritual path is easy, but the mind thinks it is rough. You need to have Love so big that you forget the mind. Your mind is always chirping; learn to ignore it.

Poetry is a song. It has musical vibrations.

When you do the work from a pure heart, it shows, and people will be attracted to it. Going within is what connects you with Source. It is so important to go within and be still with the Divine Presence.

People will move to the places on Earth that are a vibrational match. Be with Souls whom you resonate with vibrationally and you will thrive. Don't be afraid of shining your light and being powerful. Master Souls have come to Earth even though they were advised it would be a tough assignment. This was to continue their mastership training and tests to pass on their journey back to the highest octave, the Home Vibration. Humanity is being asked to hold higher levels of consciousness.

Your body will become so sensitive that there will be foods you cannot eat.

The different spiritual teachings are similar to the different flavors of ice cream.

When you are Enlightened, you have to live outside of the tribe, because you are so different. You are shunned, so you live alone. People come to you for help. One day you won't be seen as odd or strange. You will be seen as balanced.

You are trying to look at yourself as a Spiritual Being, not a Temporal Being, through thoughts, words, and action. No one can change your thoughts and actions for you. The Divine Presence can guide you, yet you are the one who has to alter your thoughts, words, and feelings.

You can live a meaningful life. You can find an opportunity to work in a place that has meaning. Use your Soul Energy to create a new life for yourself, not to create entertainment and distractions.

Move the adrenaline energy through your body for about 20 minutes. Movement of your body will get this energy out of you when upset or stressed.

Getting a hug from Source is an answer. Watch for syncretistic events in your life. Sometimes Source just wants to show you.

As the human collective wakes up and moves into higher frequencies, the Moon and Sun will look different. If you are reading this, you have already shifted and been activated.

Let go of judgment. Get lighter and start walking taller on the Earth. Honor and understand the human species. They are misled, manipulated, hurt, and angry. Look at humanity as an adult looking at a child. One day they will become adults at the right time. You are a cocreator being and a piece of Source.

Sometimes you have to come down to the lower physical realm and check on the children, the younger Souls who are still in the lower grades in the Earth School. There is no judgment; it is just an observation. A university student does not look down on the third grader; they recognize their evolutionary level. There is nothing wrong with being a third grader. The university student knows that this third grader will graduate and move into the university grade level one day. Remember your True Identity. You are a piece of Source in physical form having a human journey. You are Source wearing a human disguise. This is awareness at the level of God Consciousness. This may not be easy to accept because you created a very powerful Ego to resist all this stuff. Don't resist your Ego. Love and accept all aspects of your consciousness.

Can you see through the play with all the characters you have created? Use that energy of Source to pull all the enemies into your heart for purification. Remember all that you see is the mind, the Egoic structure that comes from consciousness. The Ego does not want to acknowledge a power that is higher than itself, so it will quickly reject a higher perspective. The Waking Dream appears real only while you are in it. Source is the Cosmic Dreamer and enjoys these adventures.

You have two choices here. Get lost and stay in the story or realize you are in a Cosmic Drama. Now create something wonderful. You don't have to burden yourself with having to figure all this out. You can just have fun here walking with your Higher Self each day. Come to your Divine Essence. Everything can be resolved by coming to Source and asking for wisdom and guidance. The enemy is just an aspect of your mind, which likes to create drama. Therefore, it creates all these villains. Heal this aspect of your mind by sending love and light to this person, then stay with the Higher Self. Be a peaceful person. Be peaceful in your own consciousness.

Until you can move beyond Duality, you can experience yourself in the Oneness. See the Beloved everywhere. The separation is the illusion. You don't deny that you are in the Waking Dream; you just stay awake and aware of it.

The mind is in Duality. Soul is in the non-Duality aspects of Source.

In the beginning of your awakening, you realize you are in captivity. There is another reality. Soul had to take on an incarnation and experience separation and feel lost. Then it awakens to realize that this life was to gain experience in the physical. You step into this life, get lost in the Waking Dream, then get awakened to see that you are in a dilemma. You are in a world of illusions, a temporary life. You are a Divine Being having a physical life. The goal is recognizing when you are in your Ego, so that you can move into your Soul. Stay in the Higher Self, so you don't get lost in this incarnation. Your curriculum is for you to awaken from the illusion of your separateness from Source.

We need to train ourselves while we are here on Earth. Our thoughts are visible and can be seen by others, such as Guardians, higher beings of light, psychics, etc. When we enter the other side, everyone can see our thoughts. It is better to train ourselves to remember until it becomes habit and becomes normal that when we discuss someone, we picture them in our presence and able to hear us. When training for spiritual mastery, everything we go through we will use to help us in guiding others who will go through similar situations. Nothing is wasted. Nothing. All situations are lessons, and we will be used for future situations with other people we will be put in charge of to guide them on their path here on the Earth. All the emotions, hurts, feelings, and situations, all of it. Do not fret, you will be able to draw from all of it.

You are a victim of your own mind. Quit identifying with it. Humor allows you to take yourself lightly.

The Dark Night of the Soul is when you realize that in order to stay awake, you have to step away from all those inducements that cause you to get lost in the Waking Dream. You are heartbroken because you feel you won't get to experience all the excitement that caused you to dive into this intense life. You realize that intensity is gone that came from being lost in the drama of life.

Mass migrations of people are fleeing violence and oppression on this planet at this time. Always look at the spiritual aspect of every situation and you will see the deeper meaning, the deeper truth of what is going on within you. Stay more with your Higher Self and be more aware of Divine Presence. There is a fleeing of your consciousness from the violence and oppression from your Ego, which are your thoughts and emotions. Understand this consciousness shift. All that is happening is happening within you. This mass migration is good! It is mass consciousness wanting freedom and liberty from the old ways of living life. They want to start anew, a fresh start in a higher level of living and a higher standard of living.

Pain is going to happen; suffering is optional.

The Shift, the Great Awakening, is where Light is greater than Darkness. This causes the human collective to wake up and remember their True Identity as Divine Beings and live a harmonious life together on this planet. There is a new energy on the Earth. More intense Light is causing the changes to occur.

The Earth School allows the Soul to Explore this play and then to awaken out of the illusion of separateness. Coming to Earth is a choice, not a punishment. Practice spending time beyond the drama.

Be okay with leaving form and going back Home. We just drop the garment of the body. It's safe, natural, and freeing. We are Source Energy Beings Individualized.

You have 7 octillion atoms in your body. Every atom is a Soul. Your Universe is your body, and all the planes are inside your cranium. On the spiritual journey, Mind, Ego, and Personality do *not* die; they are purified, then flip and look upward.

It does not matter what happens. It matters what you do with what happens. That makes all the difference.

The first stage to Enlightenment is to lighten up. Don't take things so seriously. Have some fun. Go with where the current takes you. Go with the flow. Don't swim upstream unless you enjoy pain.

When you let go of limited beliefs, you have to wash out those chemicals that hold onto those limited beliefs. We wash those out with tears. Tears of Relief, Tears of Release, and Tears of Joy. Ascendance is the raising of your frequencies.

Trust, relax, and know that no matter what happens, it will benefit you. It could take years to finally see this, yet rest in this wisdom. No matter what happens, no matter how things look, it will always benefit you. This is the position of power. This is self-empowerment. Stay with this viewpoint unless you like to suffer.

At some point, every civilization reaches a certain level of technology. They have to decide whether they are going with Artificial Intelligence (AI) technology or Consciousness-Based (CB) technology. The AI technology is machine based and has a mind of its own. The CB technology interfaces with the human biological mind. For example, a person sits in front of a computer and telepathically communicates with this electronic device. There is no keyboard and no mouse. The person telepathically thinks to the computer, and the device puts in the data. Therefore, if a person is wanting to place information on an electronic page, then the computer words will show on the screen what the person is thinking and wanting to convey in the document. You have to be at a certain high-frequency level

PROFOUND SPIRITUAL WISDOMS

in order to access and interface with this CB technology. This is why spiritual teachers will say to raise your vibrational frequency. Every person's body is a universe. You are a microcosm of the macrocosm. You have all these Souls (atoms) within your physical universe (your body). Quantum physicists have said that within each atom, there is a universe. Can you now see how profound this goes and continues? You may not be as powerful as the overall macrocosm, yet each universe is a piece of the All. The microcosm is a small reflection of the macrocosm. This is why the Human Temple is a walking reflection of Source. We have to maintain this High Frequency because every atom is a Soul. A cluster of atoms makes up a cell. A group of cells makes up an organ. If you are resonating at a higher Hertz level, it affects the whole universal body. You have a dominant frequency that you reside at most of the day. This affects your overall cosmology of your microcosm, your body, your universe. When you are at a certain frequency, the atoms, cells, and organs are vibrating at such a high frequency that telepathic abilities and other talents come online, hence the ability to unite with the CB technology. Humanity is at a turning point, and by raising their vibrational frequency, this offers the CB technology a chance to become a reality.

Who is the essence behind your eyes looking outward?

Separation is an illusion. How can one be separated when made up of 100 percent Source Energy? The Soul is a piece of the

Omnipotent Divine Essence. We are Source Individualized having a human experience. The Ego/Mind is the filter between Soul and Source. This is why the Soul in a physical form will say, "Pain is separation from the Divine." We get lost in the Ego and therefore feel this separation.

The universe is built on sound patterns. Each universe has a different frequency. That is why so many dimensions can exist and they don't see each other or know about the other universes.

You have Worth. You are Precious. You are Loved. You are a Divine Being. You are a Spiritual Master in training. I love you. I am proud of you for your strength, courage, and perseverance. Other people are just playing a role in your life. Forgive so that you can move on. Move forward with your life.

Go to the altar of joy. Source is with you. See the Divine Essence at work; see you at work on the Earth. Consciousness is also known as DNA. When you reach Mastery of each level, the DNA Codes are activated.

Anger is when you don't feel loved. Many people are missing love. Complaining is forgetting your empowerment. If or when you stop being the Light, you have fallen for the antics of the Ego. Use compassion toward other people because they could be going through a lot of things. Remember this is your mission. This is developing your skills. There is no place that Source is not. There is no place that Peace is not. There is no place that Love is not. These are the lessons. There are hostile people here on Earth. They don't know the Real Love here. The goal is to be more loving. The Lightworker is living in two worlds: the world of matter and the world of Eternity. That is what we do here on planet Earth. You don't diminish when you share infinitely. We are to be representatives of the Source Light. Your consciousness needs to be high enough to love people and to care about them. Don't be triggered by their ego and vulnerability. We need to move beyond survival and be in thrive. Know that everyone is applauding you. Don't sweat the small stuff. Understand the mission.

Exoteric Teachings are what are taught to the masses. Prayer is taught. Dogma is taught. Religion is accepted. The seeker is still not awakened to their true identity.

What is Darkness? In the beginning there was Infinite Darkness. You brought Light into this Dark world. How can you fix or clean it without experiencing it? If you are not bringing the Light to it, you end up in victimhood. Only a messed-up person would abuse another person. The ego gets hurt, not the Soul. Sometimes your Higher Self will create the storm in order for you to turn within. The difficult people were abused themselves.

Can you see them as Source sees them? It is great to learn how much we can love them, even the difficult people who were abused themselves.

Happiness is Self-Love. You can be the Light to your friends. The more you let go, the more the struggles leave. Say to the Divine Presence, "Thy Will Be Done." Surrender your life to the Divine Plan. Have people match your frequency. Find people who match your frequency. Be a living example of being healthy and living a healthy life. Learn how to practice nonreaction. We have lots of feelings, but it does not mean we have to follow these feelings. Let things happen and unfold for you. Find joy in everything you do.

A higher perspective will see that you have to feel unconditional love to understand what love is. At the level of unconditional love, you recognize that you have created everything that is around you. You love everything as it is. You may not like it, yet you are aware that from this higher perspective you can see the whole depiction. You are interfacing with yourself to have all these experiences. Judgment is when you see an experience from your perspective and you cannot see the entire picture. You are continuously being shown what needs to be integrated back into the wholeness of who you have always been. This requires a large amount of nonjudgment. You are turning on, being activated, and remembering. This is a cellular integration. Your cells are shifting into a higher frequency. It is all energy.

Soul creates diverse realities to be able to see different aspects of itself. You have created every perspective. We are projecting this reality. We are learning to love ourselves in every possible way. It is yourself from another perspective. Love all the projections of yourself. The vibration of Sound is the energy of Light. Source creates the Soul, and Soul creates the physical form. The Soul creates more experiences, and this is called Ascendance, in order to get better from every experience. Evolution is the primary cause for being.

Wisdom is not knowing the information; it is understanding the truth. The Divine cares if you have learned and evolved as a result of your experiences. The process in the universe is evolutionary Ascendance. We are evolving so we can know our true identity as an aspect of Source and can experience God Realization. When a person knows that they are a piece of Source and therefore a fully Divine Being, they are interested in the experience of God Realization.

The intensity of Light will increase on this planet and at the same time the intensity of Darkness. You are here to hold your ground and stand in the Darkness. You never run from the Darkness; you stand in it and hold your ground. While you are here on this planet, you are protected and safe. Standing in this low frequency is painful. Some days, it can be agony. Remember you are in a Waking Dream, a matrix, a hologram, and you have the ability to see through this physical illusion. It appears real while you are here experiencing it. Remember the Light you hold is more powerful than any Darkness. It cannot diminish your Light. This is why you are on this planet. You are the Lighthouse, the Lightworker, showing the way to the Light. You will find people who will be choosing which energetic field they want to live in. We see both existing in this world. You cannot separate yourself from the quantum field, for you are standing in it, all of it. You are here to master it, to choose, to remember your true identity. Stand in the chaos as an empowered Divine Light Being. You are an expression of the Divine Essence.

Set realistic expectations about perfection. Being in an Enlightened State of Being does not mean that nothing will bother you. You are in a human form, and you will experience all kinds of emotions that will be impacting you. You are here to feel and experience everything. You will feel it all. You will feel pain, suffering, evil, betrayal, corruption, and so forth. Have an absolute perception of who you are inside this physical form. This is an illusion in physicality. Master this illusion by staying awake and aware and remembering your true identity as a Divine Being in a physical form. You are the warrior of Light and came to this planet to shine.

When you are for or against something, you are in the world of duality. The world of the Ego is Duality. A spiritual student wants to get into dimensions above the Ego. The Soul gets caught in the illusion of the Waking Dream. After leaving the highest realm of Source, it travels downward into the Dream world of adventures for Self-Discovery. This is the Journey of Soul. At some point, it is time to wake up and remember Soul's true identity and see that one is in the captivity of the Ego. Once this has been discovered, the goal is to leave the dimensions of duality and travel Home. Absorption and union with Source are not loss of your unique energetic signature (individuality); it is awareness that you are a Divine Being. You are Spiritual Royalty. The Ego will whisper lies into your ears. The Ego wants to keep control over the Soul. Once a person has awakened to their true identity as a Divine Being, they move into the first position, and the Ego steps back into the second position and serves the Soul's wishes. At first the Ego will fight the Soul. In time, the Celestial Sound of the Soul soothes and spiritualizes the Ego. Once the Ego gives up the fight, it forever serves the Soul, who is only interested in serving the Divine Plan. The Ego will try to detain the Soul in the lower worlds for as long as possible. The Ego needs the energy of the Soul to survive and resents the fact that it is dependent, causing issues when trying to stay in control. Stay awake and aware of Ego's tricks to keep you in bondage to the lower realms. Staying awake in the Waking Dream is your power.

Evolutionary Ascendance of Unity. A higher level of awareness of good and bad do not exist; it sees only Unity. Understand the purpose of transcendence. The correct way is when you know that you need to transform your reality into another one. The incorrect way is when you say, "No, I don't want to change," and hence your reality is changed by force. The primary expression of the universe is Ascendance. You will shift through surrender or force. You need to be in the flow of harmony as evolving the viewpoint of your life. Find the middle path of balance. Live in harmony in every aspect of your life.

The spiritual law of acceptance offers a seeker to accept more changes in their life. As you move higher, you will have to be willing to change. These changes can appear to be not good, yet as moving onward and upward to higher ground, you need to continue forward. Challenges are part of the climb, and your Higher Self will lead you. Problems are opportunities, yet this is what the Soul requires. Work, effort, and action equal purpose work for the Divine Plan. Right view, right thought, and right action are the purification process. Do not judge these experiences in this life. The Soul says, "Let's keep moving upward." Don't get stuck in the situations, keep moving. Move, move, move, and stay going forward. Some people will not be able to keep up with you. Keep going. Your assignment is already causing you to keep going. If you could see from the level of the Higher Self, you will see things with gratitude. The Divine Presence is showing us what we need to improve in us. The spiritual path is not easy. Living your life blissfully is the ultimate goal of your life. Your life itself is the path.

Connecting with the Higher Self offers observations, wisdoms, and understanding, causing open-mindedness. If one is bound by traditions, external rites, and rituals, then they are unable to see clearly. Fighting over traditions and superstitions is as a slave to rites and rituals. The spiritual seeker should choose the real and imperative and discard the unreal and superficial. When a seeker connects to their Higher Self, they understand because they are awakened to seeing all situations from the Soul perspective.

Anything that comes and goes is not real, which is the waking state or waking dream.

Don't do something you don't like to do. Don't do what you hate. Be sincere. Have a realized life. Be aware of those who would manipulate the mind to take away what is in your heart. Have spiritual eyes to utilize only what is beneficial to you.

The individuality of the Soul wants to go out and have direct experience of life. You can only be homeschooled for so long. At some point, you need to go off and go to college. That is why the Soul leaves Source and comes to earth. The Soul has its lessons and exams in the Earth School.

Esoteric Teachings offer direct personal experience by going within to discover the hidden teachings of Self-Realization and God Realization attainment. Spiritual discipline is accomplished. The spiritual seeker rules by their own heart. All paths lead to Source.

Promote love on earth because that is wisdom and is what all the Master Souls teach. What really counts is what you did between life and death on this planet. Love is just the name we use for resonance. When we resonate to this level of love, then we can integrate with the Divine Prescence because we are at the same frequency. WE must become what you want.

Devotion is the process of harmonizing and becoming One. To remember is to Re-Member with all that is. Spiritual practice is time spent going inward to reconnect with the Higher Self. A spiritual practice quiets the mind, and the synthesis of the spirit happens. It's LOVE because consciousness loved Itself; it had no others to resonate with. The Oneness is discovered.

If you want to experience the ecstasy with Divine Love, you should engage in a spiritual practice. This allows a spiritual seeker to have time away from the ego. This helps in the process of remembering and staying connected to the Divine Presence, who is seen everywhere and in everything. Lovers listen to the inner guidance of the Higher Self and remain in communication with the Divine Essence.

Don't believe the falsehood that you are separate from Divine Source.

Divine Source says, "I want you for myself. I don't want to share you with Ego. Stay with me by keeping your attention focused on our connection."

Who am I? Where did I come from? Why am I here? Where am I going? When a person starts to ask these questions, they are now a Seeker of Truth. You need to know where you came from. This is the process of remembering.

Source pervades everywhere: in the forests, hills, rivers, deserts, and whatever place you call holy. You don't need to go anywhere; you go within the body temple for quiet and solitude. We need to control the senses to connect with the Higher Self and experience the Divine Presence internally.

The egoic mind has a tendency for otherness. A spiritual practice removes the ego and allows Soul to have union with Source. People forget the Divine and become entangled in the creation.

Those who commune with the Divine Presence lose their love of the ego. Their light is pure, and they remember their true identity and continue service to the Divine Plan.

Everything that is seen is perishable. People, houses, furnishings, cars, and their bodies are all perishable. People need to remember, for they have gotten lost in these entanglements. People are in a state of going, have gone, or getting ready to go across the veil and transition to the other side. This world is temporary. Don't waste your energy getting wrapped up with the world of the ego. Only Source and the Soul inside the body are real and eternal. What is the value of life? We should keep our attention on our spiritual goals. One of these spiritual goals is staying awake and aware of this Divine connection we have with Source Frequency.

May all living beings prosper and have peace and good fellowship. Send out good wishes for the highest and best welfare of the entire universe. Real prayer consists of wishing for the good of all.

When Soul is connected with Source, it receives infinite powers of strength. Although you are in a body, there is a power within you that is immense. This power is the Omnipotent Source. The true reality is that Soul and Source are One. Some people deny the existence of Source, who is invisible and unseen. The Divine Essence cannot be seen by the physical senses. Source permeates our Soul and is not separate from us, whether we believe this or not.

Darkness is exposed by the Power of Truth. Darkness is based on falsehood and deception. The Light of Truth exposes the lies and corruption, showing the weak side of Darkness. Vast establishments are afraid of losing their power by the awakening from ignorance. Spiritual Master Souls who have walked this planet caused awareness by revealing the highest truths to the masses. Master Teacher Souls teach us to focus on the spiritual truths and live the spiritual principles. Belief systems teach worship to a dead Master Soul Teacher and very little on applying the spiritual teachings in their daily life, much less becoming a Master Soul in their own right through achieving mastery level. A Master Soul will teach about the mastery and awareness of spiritual attainments and how to stay in these higher states of being while walking on this planet. Living above the ego and personality is a high level of mastery causing a nonduality consciousness level.

Fix what you can and leave the rest to Source.

Source dwells within and illuminates our Soul. If you need help, go within and ask your Higher Self/Soul for the highest and best outcome for you and everyone involved in the situation.

Know that the Divine is with you, is within you, and is your true essence.

There comes a stage in the spiritual path where feelings are expressed from the heart. A real yearning comes within yourself. This kindles the fire that burns away the attachment to the ego and outer world. Lovers for the Beloved produce this yearning of deep connection.

There are times when the Lightworker can get tired and wants to take a break from the conflicts of this life. The Lightworker may wish to stop their mission or purpose work for some time. After a period of time, the wave of hope and love will come and again returns to service toward the Divine Plan.

The higher the vibrational frequency of a person, the more this will offset the individuals who are at low-vibrational negative levels on this planet.

Then comes a memorable event that creates this yearning to return to this indescribable state. The seeker is now the knower and willingly gives up everything in the outer world. The seeking is replaced with surrender, action, and allegiance.

Spiritual inspiration becomes the strength that fuels one's life. All outer desires fade away compared to the highest realized state. This is the state of the Lover for the Beloved who is willing to dedicate their life into service toward the Divine Plan. This seems uncomfortable to the seeker until the mystical experience occurs. The ideal is the deep inner awareness of one's true identity as Source manifested into physical form in order to experience Itself.

Pay attention to the True Reality. Infinite Source is the True Reality; all else is a dream. You can wake up from the Waking Dream while you are in the dream state. The hard part is staying awake and aware while in the Waking Dream reality. The ego/mind complex is the veil between Soul and Source. It is a presumed separation.

Pledge your love every morning in your spiritual time alone with Source.

If someone deeply injures you in any way, allow them to stay in their darkness. You cannot fix them or change their behavior. Surrender the situation to the Divine Essence and move onward. At some point, the person will experience what you went through on the other side of the veil. After leaving this life, every person goes through Life Review. How did their life affect others? The egoic mind will play tricks and use excuses for justification, yet on the other side of life, all is revealed in the Light of Truth. Nothing is hidden from the All-Pervading Eye.

A gemologist will tell you that it has been proven scientifically that coal and diamond are both carbon, yet there is a difference in the price. Outwardly looking at humanity, people seem as human beings yet are not in reality. The Soul within is beyond price or measurement.

Source resides forever in your Soul. The entire ocean can't drown it. A forest fire can't burn it. No one can take this from you. The arrow has pierced your Soul, and the Beloved is waking you up from this dream. Sleep no more and awake from this ocean of existence. Come to the place where pain and agony will cease and you will find peace. Rarely does one find this narrow path, yet the ones who do reach this far shore. They never look at this temporary world the same way again. Give meaning to your life, connect with your infinite Divinity, and remember the Supreme Source, which will fill your Soul with joy. Only the Soul can fathom the splendor of this state of being.

Letting go of negativity brings deep emotional healing and allows for the ease in ability to read people and situations energetically. E-motions (Energy in Motion) are in constant flux and movement. Emotions are the movement of energy through the body. Spiritually evolved people are not perfect. They still get frustrated by how things are in the world; however, they stay in service to the Divine Plan. It is not a matter of bypassing; it's you choosing to focus on a higher level such as peace, kindness, completing a project, and so forth. Acceptance of emotions removes the repression of feelings. We are not choosing to stay in the negative energetic emotion. Go make yourself a cup of tea or coffee, drive or walk to the market, listen to fun music, and see how fast the negative energetic emotionally charged energy moves out. We all have the ability to master our emotions. What causes the issue is the intense flow and influence of the energy attached to the feeling being experienced. These emotions come and go. Acknowledge the emotion and allow the energy to flow through you, whether negative or positive. Everyone experiences these energetic states of being. You just don't want to hold onto them. Allow them to flow through your body and then let them go.

It is the ego that makes us feel that this outer reality is real. This outer world is like an amusement park. It is the wise Soul who chooses to go inward and connect to the real joy that the Divine has to offer them.

Source's music is the primordial sound, the unstruck symphony, and eternal power of creation. Countless Souls are awakened upon hearing the celestial harmonic frequencies. The Beloved is beyond names or forms, the origin of everything; it existed before creation and continues throughout eternity. The Beloved leaves home, takes on form, gathers the Souls that are ready, and reminds them of a long-forgotten realm. Your ship has come in. Don't delay. Step on board to become awakened and free yourself from rituals, fear, and this dream—many for which it has become a nightmare. Supreme Source's voice of the sound current is calling you home and calling you to remember your origin. You have played in the playground of existence for so long and now are being called back home. You are Divine Beings and need to remember your Divinity. Retrace you journey toward your original home. It helps to sing along the path toward home. You are very close, and you don't have far to travel. The only veil between you and home is the world of the ego.

What is the goal? Ultimate Awareness. The True Self is all that is. The Source within pervades all and Is All.

We are caught in the agony of Ego's web. The escape is to drop the sense of our separate existence. Source offers Free Will; therefore, we can ignore or accept the loving offer to connect with the eternal spring of Divine Love. There is always room available at this banquet. You can drink the poison of this temporary world, or you can partake in the ambrosia of the Divine treasure. Those who have been awakened are connected to the Divine Presence. Connect your hearts to the Beloved and end the agony of Ego's web. The pain of separation is so intense it anguishes constantly. We fill it with temporary delights, yet nothing fills this starvation. The planes of existence are worthless to us. It is like a knife stabbing at our hearts. Nothing compares to the ceaseless celestial melody of Source Frequency. Absorption, love, and reverence allow us to lose our connection with this temporary world, and yet we have been asked to serve humanity and help them remember their divinity.

You are here in physical form so you can have a fuller understanding of Light and Darkness, emotions, Soul's individuality, an accomplishment of goals, the experience of time, space, matter, and so much more. What if a Soul wants to experience giving birth to a new life? Then one has to take on a physical form. They may want to experience swimming in the ocean with all the different forms of sea life. There are many reasons why a Soul will choose to incarnate into a physical form. You may have been asked to be tested and prove or improve your abilities before your next assignment in your next incarnation. Ego has one way of looking at things, yet the Soul has a much higher perspective as to why we are to go through situations.

Unfoldment comes in each moment. You have within you the resources to handle every experience. Your Soul is very powerful, and you chose to yield to circumstances knowing that the Waking Dream would be temporary. Your True Essence, your True Self, can never be harmed. Here you are on the Earth dealing with all sorts of situations you never expected. Maybe you did? In the far reaches of Eternity, we experience the pain and the joy. You chose to step away from Infinite Bliss to experience the human journey. For many, this Waking Dream has been a nightmare. Knowing your True Identity as a piece of Source, a Soul, in human form, will offer you the opportunity to feel your power. You can overcome the negative thought loop within yourself. Continue to move beyond and connect with your Higher Self. With training and practice, you can feed yourself a healthy thought diet and make peace with your past. Your Light is so vast. Your walking through the Darkness exposes your Divinity, power, and authority. When you step to the other side of life, you will know you are a Divine Being. Your viewpoint about your situations needs to be seen from a higher perspective. The human collective has lost so much on the outer, yet you can't lose yourself. These openings create space for something new. You are more powerful than you realize. Your brilliant Light is stunning! Remember that this Waking Dream in Duality is temporary. Know Thyself as Divinity. You are the sacred Essence of Source.

You can't even imagine the vastness inside you. Huge regions are waiting for you to explore. Keep going so you can see them. Keep moving forward in your self- discovery.

Awakening to your Divinity is only the beginning. You are experiencing a holographic reality called the Waking Dream. You perceive this reality to be real and the only one, yet there are many levels of realities. This is the world of the Ego that rules over the Essence of the Soul. Your Ego covers your True Identity. The wise want to see their powerful Divinity. You have Free Will to choose the Light and conquer Darkness. Go within to this place of peace. You are the collective Divinity of the One Divine Source.

To know of our Divinity and union with Source is greater than all the collected wealth in the world.

The answers are within you; what is needed is access to them. Life can be a rollercoaster ride when really you enjoy and wish for a peaceful existence. Here you are thinking peace has left you when actually the wild ride has overturned your emotions. Try not to let the louder emotions drown out the softer harmonic tones of joyfulness. You can go through life in search of this celestial music filled with bliss. This Divine melody is within you, just waiting for you to turn inward to experience it, at any time. Joy is the path. It is within your Soul. At any moment, you can tap into this abundance of jubilation. Take time often to free your heart from the burdens and feel this exuberance of Divine Love that is so portable because you carry it within. There is no shortage, and it is available for everyone. Go to a memory when you experienced enjoyment. It is free to delight in. The more joy you give away, the more it grows. Everyone is hungry for happiness. Even animals enjoy being happy. Why does sadness exist? How else would you know the true treasure of joy, peace, and love? You must have knowledge of all the emotional states.

Even when in grief and despair, your Soul reminds you through memories of laughter and cheer. A single memory can turn your life around. There is a frequency assigned to each emotion. Take a cup and dip into your reservoir of blissful love.

No amount of human technology can replace our Higher Self because Soul is the Source within us. The Higher Self is spiritual technology. Let us not rely completely on human technology to solve all our collective problems. An example of consciousness-based technology is telepathic communication abilities. The Soul is aligned with Source and therefore offers higher consciousness to be used for the advancement of the human collective.

You are on a magnificent journey of self-discovery. You launch into a reality of the unknown to learn valuable lessons in the Earth School, to overcome challenges, to experience corruption, to awaken to the wisdom where transformation occurs and a rebirth sets you onward toward your return home. You have your own unique journey. Continue moving forward, even if it feels as if your path has become steep and you are on the side of a mountain. A small step is movement forward. This journey is about you. Upon return home, you have been transformed and understand deeper that you are Divine Royalty. You are a Divine Being, pretending to be human on this journey in a physical reality. Remembering your true identity is the transformation of your consciousness.

All that you need is within you. God Realization is not that far off; it is right within you. It's like saying to the child that adulthood in within them. The child has everything they need within to grow into adulthood. You already have everything you need inside. Stay connected to the Divine Presence. When the Ego acts up, stay at peace with the Higher Self.

As long as there is an Ego, you cannot experience Self-Realization and God Realization. This is why it is talked about, for the ego has to be moved aside and then the realizations are revealed. This can happen in stages or all at once, depending upon the spiritual student. The Soul is independent of the Ego. When the Soul moves beyond the confines of the Ego, it remembers its Divinity and Oneness with the Infinite Source. The Soul has forgotten and thought it was just a human being when, in fact, it is a Divine Being.

When someone is mean and hurtful, know that their ego/mind is torturing them. Try not to react and stay calm. It is only the mind and ego that are sensitive and reacting.

The goal of a spiritual path of love is to become one with the Self and God. What is standing in the way is the Ego. If you are on a spiritual path of love, you must learn to develop your inner life, your inner connection with the Divine Presence that is within you at all times. We tend to get lost in this outer life so much that we forget our inner life. A deep spiritual path is about balance between the inner life and the outer life.

There is widespread loneliness on this Earth. When a person identifies with their Ego, which is their false sense of identity, this results in feeling separate and alone. While being in physical form, we are in the world of the Ego. This feeling of separateness is caused by this illusion of the Ego, which is the barrier between Soul and Source. Soul cannot be separate from what it is made of and therefore has constant union. The pains of separation from Source are very real, and the intensity can be felt many times throughout the day depending upon what we are going through while in this life. This is why it is very important to develop a spiritual practice or at least set aside time each day to connect with your Higher Self, which is in constant union with Source. Time in union with Source helps because you visit home for a while. It is bittersweet, for you are so happy and feel deeply loved yet know that you will have to step back into the physical dimension to play in the separation for further evolution. You can go to visit home at any time. This will help in staying awake and aware that while you are in the Waking Dream, you can know this is temporary, as if you have gone off to a distant school away from home. Many Souls know this Earth is not their home of origin, and they feel homesick. When you feel alone, try to go within to connect to the Divine Presence. Many times a day you can step outside the ego identity. Remember that you are a

Soul, and remember your true identity. Remember that you are temporarily away at a distant school yet can call home by connecting through contemplation or the many different spiritual practices available. Each person is unique, and whatever provides you this connection is all that matters. The Divine Presence is within you, and you can call home at any time to connect, feel loved, and get encouragement to keep going. Remember to pick up the spiritual phone to call home when you feel alone or overwhelmed. A spiritual community also helps, for we all need connection on the outside, and hugs from friends do wonders for homesickness.

There are Souls that are in conflict and under the spell of illusion. They will not understand the evolved and awakened Souls. Try to remember to look at people as Souls and not mere human beings. Most people are caught up in the illusion of separateness. The Awakened Souls see the Oneness of Source within themselves and the same Divine Presence within all. As you travel further along the spiritual path, you will be more of an observer of life instead of emotionally involved in situations. Know that Source's Divine Presence guides you through the illusions of separateness and your journey moves you to Absolute Oneness. There are love and oneness, and then there are separateness and loneliness. Evil is based on extreme separateness. Each Soul chooses to move closer to Light/Source or away through ill-thought-out causes due to their Free Will toward Darkness/Separation. In the absolute reality, there is Source and Oneness. In the dimensions of duality, we have Free Will to choose in this temporary physical plane of existence. Each Soul comes into the illusion so they may awaken to have a life of understanding the Divine Presence within All and that IS All.

Keep the Divine Remembrance or awareness that this is an illusion, for when removed, only Source exists.

What is more glorious than service to the Divine Plan?

Remember that the unawakened Souls are unaware of their effects on others and forgive them for their ignorance. Many of Earth's residents are in the initial stage of reawakening. They don't understand that their patterns are destructive. Only the awakened Souls know that the path of peace, love, and balance is the way to eternal Oneness with the Divine Presence. Rise above the drama and walk a Divine inspirational life.

Along the spiritual path at some point, the personal ego gets put aside and is replaced with the Soul leading the life of the individual. This brings a deeper acceptance of their human journey, harmony, and balance. In the beginning, there is this movement of internal acceptance and union, and then it is pulled outward by the physical senses. This back and forth between Ego and Soul is normal. Over time, it becomes less, and while a person goes through their day, they stay in the remembrance of their true identity of a Divine Being having a human journey. We need to know that the Supreme Presence is always in power and has the highest good for every Soul. The major exams in the Earth School can be extremely overwhelming. When these tests come, how we handle them demonstrates our fortitude and strength toward our service to the Divine Plan. The key is to keep moving forward, even if it is with small steps. You eventually get to the top of the mountain. Upon arrival, the much higher viewpoint changes your perspective. The viewpoint at the top of the mountain is much superior to the one held while standing at ground level.

When one encounters religious zealots, it is best to remain silent and allow the people to talk and then excuse yourself quickly. Why waste your energy talking with them when they are convinced and deep into separation? Know that possibly in this lifetime or in a future lifetime, they will awaken to higher spiritual truths.

Aware Souls focus their life on serving the Divine Plan by releasing the personal will for the Divine Will.

Earthly life is exhausting. The physical senses control the Ego identity, where even the Ego gets tired of all the drama. Then the Ego becomes ready to go inward and let the true power of the Soul run the overall life with all the situations. This is a big step in the spiritual journey. When a person comes to know their true identity that they are a piece of Source and therefore always connected, they go inward to enjoy this ultimate oneness and love. There is more to experience than the physical realm. You can't stay in these higher dimensions while in physical form, yet you can visit them and reconnect with your true essence. The final level is absorption into the Divine Presence. This means your attention is absorbed with Source Essence, where you don't forget your true identity as a Soul, a Divine Being.

The closer you are to Source, the further away you are from illusions that separate.

There are rare high levels that share the message of the spiritual path to help the Soul groups that are lacking the awareness of the Divine Presence within that is love.

We are experiencing a collective neurosis in a dysfunctional society. What is up is down and what is down is up. The best that psychologists and psychiatrists can do is help people to function in a dysfunctional society. The illusions and trends of our present-day society are considered the skill to function within the dysfunctional collective. Psychology and psychiatry view the personal ego and the identity as the self. Placement of many egos together creates an ego society. Mental health professionals help people become functional within the collective thinking or neurosis of the modern ego society. The ego identity is perpetuated, which causes conflict and division. Then there are those who are the enlightened ones, who step out of society or remove themselves as much as possible because they recognize the dysfunction. Greed, judgment, jealously, betrayal, and hatred are some of the forms of mental illness that are dysfunctional, to name a few. There are Souls that move to an eco-community, an ashram, a spiritual community, or any other community where the Divine Consciousness can be expressed. Enlightened Souls know themselves to be unique expressions of Source, and this is their present reality. They do not serve rules that don't benefit the whole of life that lives on this planet. The Enlightened Souls are seen as unusual, odd, and misunderstood. In an Enlightened society, no court system is needed; there are no police, no religion exists, and this is filled with master-level spiritual Souls, for they recognize that they are a piece of Source and their personal will is service to the Divine Will. We currently have a society of inwardly fragmented, personally ego-centered identities in a temporary physical life. Enlightened Souls see this life as an opportunity for service to the Divine Plan, Soul growth, and true identity of oneness with Source.

The big questions and quest for meaning begin to be asked when events in a person's life are filled with pain, misery, and sorrow. Am I being tested? Do I need to experience misery in order to appreciate joy? Why am I here? Where did I come from? What is my purpose work? What happens when I die? Did I have any goals to accomplish in this life? Many questions arise, and the quest for meaning begins the expedition. At the end of the journey, a person will maintain a remembrance that this is an illusion or Waking Dream, for when removed, only Source exists, hence the recognition of their true identity. You are a piece of Source in physical form having a human experience. You are a Divine Being. Source must create in order to express through Its creations. We are all Source's expressions. Your life is Source's creation and love for you.

Rituals are needed until the person awakens to realize they interfere with further spiritual evolution. The higher awareness will cause them to view rituals as keeping them from achieving spiritual goals and attainments.

God Realization is a state of being.

Truth sets us free from the sense of the personal ego identity in order for the Soul to remember its Oneness with Source.

A true spiritual teacher will teach students of their own divinity. Go within to connect to your Higher Self, the Soul. The utmost spiritual experience will occur within the seeker. The teacher guides and is a mentor, teaching and explaining to the student that they can connect and listen to the inner guidance system of the Soul. The direct mystical experience is the ultimate teacher within you. High-level teachers are here to raise the consciousness of those on Earth who are ready to go into higher states of being. It is Source within the spiritual teacher that attracts the Souls that are ready to remember and Source that provides the instruction. The spirit guides of each Soul will guide them to the highest-vibrational spiritual teacher to receive the highest frequency in order to raise their consciousness level.

Most Souls on Earth are not awake to a high level of consciousness. It is important to get to a level where a person can see through the duality of physical life, this temporary reality, and to see from a higher consciousness level. Earth is a dimension of dualism or opposites, where pain and pleasure, love and hate, war and peace, day and night exist. Living from a higher state of being provides pure love through connection with the Higher Self, which spills over to all life on the planet.

Higher-level Souls that serve the Divine Will incarnate and know their mission prior to incarnation into physical form. While on Earth, they have an Awakening of their assignment, why they came here, and their goals. This is not a personal choice since they are in Oneness with the Divine's Will; therefore, it is Source that makes the choice. These Higher Light Hierarchs come from the Cosmic University to teach and help awaken the ready Souls for total awakening. Some Souls will only awaken partially, yet a Master Soul will do all they can to help them understand the deeper wisdoms of Cosmic Consciousness, Nonduality, Self-Realization, God Realization, and Spiritual Evolution.

See and know that All is Source manifesting in many different forms. Once Source has individualized as a Soul, it only appears to have separated from Oneness with the Divine and feels it has an individual identity. Source cannot create anything separate from Itself. There is only an appearance of separateness.

Every Soul is experiencing multiple dimensions simultaneously and having lifetimes in different timelines. Everything exists concurrently and in unison. The Soul is so vast and powerful that it has many lifetime experiences at once. You are multidimensional; therefore, you can be in many dimensions gaining different experiences.

When a person has the experience of the ego death (false sense of identity of personal ego temporarily removed), the Soul is able to experience Oneness and connection with the Supreme Source. It is the Ego that is the barrier to Oneness with Divine Love. The less the personal ego, the more the Divine Presence. To know your true identity is to understand that you are a unique expression of Absolute Source and accept that this temporary physical life is a Waking Dream. We are the Divine's Will individualized.

One of the goals is to be a reflection of the Divine Presence that is within. Even though you are in the covering of the flesh, let the Divine shine through you. Allow your luminescence to reflect the Beloved that is always with you and is you.

A higher ultimate reality is possible. After the Awakening occurs, your personal will is influenced by the Divine Will. At this higher state of being, your days are filled with more service to the Divine Plan. The outward life will appear different, even though your family life is there; the bills are there; sexuality, sickness, health, and life's responsibilities are still there. However, the ego is no longer in charge and running your life. The awakened person is guided by the Divine Presence. "Thy Will Be Done" is the new motto and expression.

Beautiful Souls, you have incarnated onto an adversarial planet to help with raising the consciousness level of the human collective, asleep as to their true identity. Do the best you can to live in this Waking Dream, or, as others have called it, a matrix, in a way that allows you to follow your heart. Do what brings you joy. Connect with others whom you resonate with and who are supportive of your spiritual path. You walk and live among a species that is unaware of their Divine nature, their spiritual royalty, their origin of Oneness with Source. Know that you are with the Divine Presence, the Beloved, at all times.

Souls need something that they can relate to on this physical plane. This is why Master Souls incarnate and help in the awakening process of other Souls who are still asleep in this Waking Dream.

Any religion that puts women in roles that are of lower importance and value and that puts men at a higher level is a hierarchy. Men and women are created equally by Source, for ALL Souls are Energetic in Origin.

Some days you will yearn for your home of origin. Remember this physical life is a temporary exploration in illusion. You cannot be separate from that which you are made of. You are a Divine Being, a piece of Source.

You are the wave, and Source is the ocean. You are the plant, and the Divine is the soil. You are the bird, and the cosmic supreme is the sky. You are the instrument, and the Divine Symphony

Concert Master is the melody. You are the radiant star, and the Celestial Essence is the universe. You are a Divine Being, and the Divine Presence is in the human temple.

By service to the Divine Plan, a person's face is always toward the Divine Presence. To be absorbed is to focus your life on the Beloved. The lover who is patiently waiting for you is the Beloved, who has barrels of love to overwhelm you in.

In the lower dimensions, all is temporary and illusory, which serves as a school for Soul to realize its Oneness with Source.

Love is the shortcut to the Divine Essence. Divine Love is eternal, while other types of love perish with time. We crave this permanent love. This creation is to know Source's love for Itself. The goal is for each Soul to be active in personifying a higher state of being. Accessing spiritual powers will help you on your spiritual path. The secret is continual connection to the Beloved Divine Presence. Spiritual exercises help keep this remembrance, which causes a purification of the ego. The Soul loses interest in the dazzle of the world, causing the senses to pull away when seeing the emptiness, temporary, and illusion. Now the Soul is free from the bondage of the senses. The captivity caused the separation and now is free to immerse itself in the Oneness of spiritual union. This cannot be forced; it can only be cultivated. There will be a moment when the Divine Union occurs.

You become that which you love.

The impression of the Divine Essence places you on a quest of union with the Beloved. You come to remember your union was never broken; the ego was the only obstacle. Arrive to the awareness to view your pure, dazzling essence. When Source rules your heart, there is profound connection.

It is the ego that is afraid of losing something it cherishes or needs to keep for support in this temporary existence that may be removed. You are experiencing the land of the ego that tries to keep your attention away from the fact that this is only a temporary school. The ego tries to trick us and make us believe we are away and separate from Source. Once Soul awakens to learn of its Divine nature, it quickly soars home to reacquaint itself with its true identity, a piece of Source. This is why the Soul is eternal and immortal and is pure energetic luminosity. A Master Soul will teach of this separate ego and the ability to ascend out of this deception through absorption on the spiritual path of union with Divine Love. Our life can be lived through the ego or Divine Love. Once the Soul is freed from the ego, it loses its fear of the temporary, for the absolute truth of Divine

Love is inextinguishable. The Soul lives in freedom, and the ego lives in fear and bondage. Divine Love is the elixir that cures this mental state of fear.

A true spiritual teacher will expose your delusions and cause you to stay with truth. The highest purpose is realization of your own divinity. You are One with Source, for you are made of this Omnipotent Supreme Essence. Source is not hidden; it pervades everything. It is the mind that tries to conceal the Divine Essence in everything.

The mind likes to label everything as good or bad because it is dual in nature. The Soul views from a higher perspective and sees everything as an experience.

The evolution of consciousness is the true change that allows one to see beyond the realms of mind and matter. The only way to get to the higher states of being is by keeping an eye on your ego. Many people are so immersed in their ego that they can't get beyond it; hence, the price is too high to leave it, meaning ego death and being able to see what is on the other side beyond the ego. Spiritual attainments are so high that the highest price must be paid, and this entails your time, energy, and separation from your ego. The barrier between Soul and remembering its Divinity is the ego, which is why the ego is recognized as the temporary illusion of separation. The sincere spiritual student will gladly give up their time, attention, ego, and entire life to attain this ocean of connection. Desire only the Divine Beloved. Lower desires are steeped in pain and separation. Strive for the highest and seek the connection with the Divine Presence.

The mind sustains the principle of duality. Soul wants to step outside of time and matter to experience the union with the Divine Essence. The mind holds the Soul in captivity. The senses hold the mind in captivity. This is why it is important to release our attachments so we can allow the Soul to have this union and remembrance with the Divine Presence. You already have the transcendent realities within you. It is about remembering what you already have. A Master Soul comes into your life to remind you of your Divine qualities. You are being called, and it is time to remember. Spiritual liberation is freedom from your mind creations. Mind enjoys playing in the creation. Soul delights in creating and has the creative power.

States of consciousness move constantly, depending upon what you are thinking about, feeling, and experiencing. There are different levels of consciousness, and that is why there are so many that we can move into and encounter. Your attention will focus on a situation, an object, emotions, and thoughts, allowing you to select the vibrational level of a particular state of consciousness. The Soul is the consciousness itself. All other states are pieces of the whole. States of consciousness are like slices of a loaf of bread. Consciousness is the entire loaf of bread. Connecting with the Higher Self, the Soul, is linking at a level beyond all the states of consciousness.

When you jump into the Ocean of Divine Love, you will never leave. You enjoy your swimming and are completely content with this infinite sea. You will spend the rest of your life trying to explain it to others. You will find that most people are content with the physical objects of this temporary Waking Dream.

Have you graded your own spiritual effort? If should be at an A level. If you would give yourself a lower grade, then continue with your homework. You are the one who is in control of your spiritual life.

The purpose of any spiritual path is to offer you the opportunity to experience the awareness that you are a Soul, a Divine Being, and a piece of Source and that this higher reality is real to you.

Learn to step outside your mind to be able to connect to your Higher Self, the Soul. Develop a spiritual practice to allow connection and remember that you are a Divine Being in a physical form. This life can swallow up all your attention so no time is left, and therefore we get trapped in the temporary illusion. Yes, the Earth School has a lot to teach us, yet we can get lost in recess and stay in the playground too long. Then you mistakenly identify with being this small human form. You are a Divine Being in a human being form.

Is your battery low on your love phone? Charge the battery, and then you will be able to make calls to the Divine Essence within you. Spiritual exercises charge the battery and allow for the calls to go through clearly. You have all the spiritual technology.

The mind seeks pleasures in the physical realm. The Soul desires realization of the truth of its own identity and Oneness with Source. We get our Divine Essence from Source, hence our Divinity. We are eternal Divine Beings. Our goal is to keep the remembrance of our true Divine Identity. It is the mind that causes Identity Theft, having us believe we are only human beings when, in fact, we are Divine Beings in a human form.

Use these contemplations to spiritualize your mind. It is much easier to work with your mind than to go in to battle and fight your mind. Your mind was made to think, so trying to shut down your mind is the struggle. Work with your mind instead of conflict by reading spiritual material, which brings peace and calmness instead of discord and friction.

Other Souls in the past have earned spiritual attainments; thereupon, you can succeed as well. In the beginning, there will be ups and downs when connecting with the Divine Presence. As you expand, this will gradually diminish, causing more of a consistent connection and awareness. This is a way of life. Spiritual unfoldment never stops. We are always expanding into infinity.

Let the mind vent, then move on quickly. Let others' minds vent, then move away from them quickly or say nothing. Move on quickly!

The spiritual path is easy; it is the mind that makes it difficult. It is the ego that complains. The enemy is the ego, for it does not want to be reined in and controlled, always wanting to roam free. The ego does not want to be held accountable for its actions. How can a spiritual student get anywhere with an undisciplined mind? It is the mind that is difficult, not the path. A true spiritual teacher knows that this takes time, and they are patient with their students. As a spiritual student continues on the path, there are new perceptions and revelations that come in and need to be integrated, embraced, and accepted. Sometimes the student feels the pace is too slow, yet staying in the awareness of these exalted states of being takes time. Anything that is quickly gained is easily lost. The child wants to become an adult overnight, yet adulthood takes time. Some students grow faster than others, which has to do with the intensity for spiritual unfoldment.

Try to remember real from unreal and illusion from truth. The real and truth are absolute. The unreal and illusion are relative truths. Absolute truth is beyond the realm of duality. Relative truth requires duality; for example, a person understands day relative to experiencing night.

There have been many powerful archangels over the ages who have chosen to incarnate into a human form without becoming famous so they could serve at a deeper level within humanity on Earth to help in the elevation of human consciousness. Higher Light Beings provide absolute service to all life. They serve the Divine Plan with strength and perseverance through love and compassion. Archangels chose to be clothed in flesh in service to humanity. Be aware of the crowd of Souls surrounding you with love. Here you are on this planet. Your Soul guides you in this life. Take a deep breath. Know that you can tap into Divine Love and it is available in every moment. Allow the love that pervades you to comfort you. Love is in everything, even the tears and moments when you feel alone. In the highest truth, you are never alone. The feeling of separation causes you to go within. This is your refuge of peace as you connect with your Soul. Remember the greatest love is within. Nothing on the outer compares to the sacred connection with your Soul. You are here on the Earth, and you have a great purpose. Your heart may have grown weary on your journey. Never give up, for there is always the path of Divine Love to be found.

Before all the religions, there was the Diving Essence that created all the Souls. Going within offers awareness to see our Divinity and frees us from all forms of religious worship. Nothing compares to the deep connection through Divine Love. It is the superpower of love that will bring you all the way back to your home of origin. The spiritual ascension is only through the power of love. It is love that comforts the heart, controls the ego, governs the senses, raises our states of consciousness, and brings us in union with the Divine Presence within. Stay connected through Divine Love, which is the power behind spiritual ascension.

Why are you still here? Because your lessons have not been completed and your purpose work is still in process.

A path is called mystical or esoteric because people are unable to understand the deep spiritual mysteries. They try to understand it with their mind, yet it is the ego that is the barrier. A person needs move beyond duality and illusion that the mind creates to awaken to unity consciousness and experience the Oneness. The mind will say, "This is impossible, for what is higher than me?" Then the Soul steps up and says, "Soul Power!" The Soul understands the wisdoms and reality of the Absolute realm. Soul can see through the veil of illusion. The mind has the ability of concealing the truth, thus keeping the mystery unsolvable. Slide the ego aside, then a person can see through the veil of illusion. The true religion is discovering one's true identity as a Soul, a piece of Source, and thereupon a Divine Being.

Practicing the Presence is Divine Love and your love for the Divine. Be transformed like the caterpillar to the butterfly. Divine Love has no restrictions. Most of humanity lives in the polarities of duality consciousness, moving between the two extremes constantly. When a person becomes awakened and embraces Truth Consciousness, they move toward unity.

You can spend your life fighting the passions. The spiritual journey is not about battling with the passions of the mind, such as anger, greed, pride, vanity, and so forth. Rather, stay with the indwelling Divine Presence within you and this love affair will bring you up. Your love will conquer these passions by keeping you at an evolved state of being. You can let the passions play out; just don't spend all day drowned in them and stay fastened with the mind. You are not the one getting upset; it is your ego. If you stay in the mind, you will forget your identity and that you are this glorious Divine Being called the Soul.

The human temple contains Source, and that is why great care should be taken of it, for it is a pristine temple. Outer temples are for the ego and the mind. Some spiritual seekers require the spiritual temples in the beginning, which help them with the spiritual fundamentals. As one advances on the path, they go inward to access the inner higher dimensions.

We have this chain of events that takes place. The Soul is bound by the mind, the physical senses are controlled by the outside things that we are attracted to, and desire attracts us to the outside world. This keeps us being trapped in this illusion or, some may say, the matrix. To reverse this, we need to recognize what is actually taking place. Then a person can loosen up on their attachments. When the Soul is awakened and remembers its high calling, the attachments start to lose their grip. The Soul steps into first position, and the ego moves into second position, allowing the Soul to take the active role. The mind begins to give up the resistance and releases the amusements, offering freedom to enjoy the Divine Essence within.

Once the Soul incarnated into the physical form and took on the mind, it forgot its true identity. When one is able to see beyond the ego, they can know their true identity firsthand through direct mystical experience. The Soul then remembers and finds comfort while functioning in the remaining time in physical form.

The competition is over the attention of the Soul, for the senses, the ego, the personality, and so on, because they are in constant movement.

What is being offered is of a much higher value than the desire of objects in the physical world. When the mind gets a taste of the Divine Presence, it gladly surrenders and takes a back seat and serves the Soul. Up to this point, the Soul is trapped by the mind, which is trapped by the senses and by the desires to connect with novelties. In the beginning, it seems fun, until after a while life begins to fade and a search for meaning happens.

The path is within you. Stay with the Divine Presence and walk the path together.

How can any spiritual student anticipate a transformation if they don't apply the spiritual principles? Soul is a piece of Source Frequency, and the communion is on the inner. Stepping onto a high spiritual path causes an awakening where unawareness is dispelled and Oneness is seen. A person lives from the heart, and the path home is revealed. Home is the blissful love ambrosia that never runs out, and one can connect to enjoy this at any moment. The purpose of life is now illuminated, knowing of their true identity and service to the Divine Plan. The Soul is a foreigner in a foreign physical land and desires to wake up from its slumber to remember its true identity as a piece of Source. Soul desires union with its true essence and craves this joyous unification.

You are a Divine Being, and you have the power to upgrade your state of consciousness. Take moments to step away from your outer life and reconnect to remember your celestial nature. You incarnated into a physical form to experience a human life. It's about reconnection with that which we already are.

See the Divine Presence with you at all times and in all places.

Your life can be a living and walking meditation. Keeping your high state of being throughout the day causes this level of consciousness to be sustained. Even the ego can get tired of constant stress and disappointments. The Soul awakens from the Waking Nightmare to see all the conundrums caused by the ego. Soul starts to clean up all the situations that hold one down in a lower state of being.

The mind and ego naturally want relief from problems, the constant stream of desires, loneliness, and lack of meaning that come from the human condition. As our consciousness ascends and experiences the impact of the blissful Divine Presence, it will forever change the person's life. Now one begins to realize that they are in captivity of the mind and ego. The spiritual path of Divine Love offers the power of living from the heart, not the intellect. The spiritual downloads and realizations keep coming in for the awakening and remembering of the true identity of divinity for the Soul. Once the Soul has reawakened and remembers, the impact is so profound that God Realization is experienced.

A child has one way of seeing things, not realizing that once adulthood is reached, the viewpoint is no longer going to be the same. You begin to feel this separateness fade away as Unity Consciousness moves into the forefront. You begin to move from desires and become this very essence of higher consciousness, for the Soul already owns everything.

It is the rebellious ego that puts up a fight because it knows at some point, the Soul gets wise to the antics of the mind. The ego is used to running the show on the physical plane, and it does not want to give up its dominion. The Soul is put in the back seat and has to go through all the nightmares and crazy situations. Then one day, a Master Soul comes along and says, "You are not your mind. You are a Divine Being, a Soul, and you don't have to live like this anymore." This ego is the problem, for it runs all over creation trying to make itself happy with the physical senses, yet this is only temporary happiness. You want permanent joy, bliss, and love that only the Soul has because it is made from the Infinite Source. Soul needs to come out of the back seat and be put in the driver's seat and take the wheel of your life. Until the Soul is the one driving your life, you will experience a wild, insane, erratic ride. Keep company with your True Self, your Soul, not your ego, and you will experience a smoother ride filled with stable guidance.

The path is very broad because it is constantly expanding to include the entire creation. The goal is liberation from the mind and ego because this is the illusionary barrier between Soul and Source. It is only the mind that makes us feel separate from the Supreme Source. Soul only feels separate while in the human temple. You cannot be separate from what you are made of, which is the Absolute Divine Source. You are already one with Source; you just have your mind lying to you. Stop listening to the whispers of your ego. Connect by taking some time each day to engage in the many forms of spiritual practices so you can remember your Divinity. Feel this bliss, love, and companionship. Practicing the Presence means remembering the Divine Presence Within you. You begin to experience this total immersion, and the Divine Love rises from within. You have it already! You just need to access and remember what you already are, which is Pure Divine Essence.

You can talk with your Higher Self all day long. This is the best companion and truest friend and offers the best counsel. You don't have to hang out with your Ego all day. You get to choose:

Ego or Soul. All that is required is application of discipline in a person's life. Trust me, Soul is the better choice. Soul always has the highest and best interests for you. You need to tell your Ego, "Get off the throne! My Soul needs a place to sit." The Ego wants to hold on tightly to rulership. It's time to tell the Ego to step aside so the Soul can take control and calm down all these stormy situations in your life. Mastership is keeping the Ego in check and maintenance of Soul custody of your attention. The Soul is the one that provides true support for you. The Ego loves drama. The Soul enjoys peace and serenity.

Please be advised that you will fall in love and will want to be close to the Divine Presence, even beyond what you can presently imagine. At the highest level of spiritual communication, you can still want to be even closer. Your yearning will push you to the level desiring to merge completely.

You are one with the Infinite Absolute Being of Source. You existed before the Earth was created. You are part of One Divine Consciousness. You arrived on Earth for a purpose. You are worth way beyond what you know currently. You came here to see beyond duality, this illusion, and know your Divinity. Let your personal story go. It is just a story you are experiencing in this Waking Dream. You can focus on what is happening now in this moment that most likely has nothing to do with what has happened in the past. Do you want peace? Give up your personal story and attachment to the painful past. What you think causes your mood and behavior. Your Higher Self has the power to stay in connection and awareness of your true identity as a piece of Source. Move your awareness to your inner existence as you walk through life.

Never compare yourself to another. The Soul sees no one greater or lesser. Only the Ego creates these distinctions. Knowing your true identity and divinity within others, you see all as ensouled and stand equally. The Ego will perceive others at a low level when, in fact, you can't always tell how high or low a person is in spiritual advancement. We should not focus on another's level when it is most prudent to center on personal ascent. We are all on our journey of evolution and self-discovery. Let us all take refuge in the expansion of our consciousness with remembering that as a piece of Source, you are infinite. When you see your true identity, you are only concerned with Oneness while retaining your own unique individuality.

While we are in physical form, our consciousness can stay at the human consciousness level or can be elevated to a higher level of consciousness. We travel in consciousness to the higher dimensions. Consciousness is not restricted and can travel anywhere. Soul can reside on any plane of existence. Even in physical form, you can travel to the higher dimensions and experience spiritual attainments. Master Souls appear similar to you, for everyone must live in a body on the physical dimension; however, they have reached a higher level of consciousness. These Souls can be talking with you while living from the God Realization state. They teach the truth of the Oneness and how Soul is the essence of Source.

While walking on the spiritual path, don't be surprised if you find that your ego is trying to sabotage your progress. Eventually, the ego calms down and gets on board with the spiritual quest. Stay close to the Divine Presence to keep the ego in check. The ego can convince you to leave the spiritual pursuit because it likes being in total control. Keep an eye on the ego, and when it acts up, let the Soul, which has the true power, provide guidance in your life.

Home is the conscious level that you are always with Source.

True Oneness involves leaving the ego altogether.

You are Light expressed into form. The consciousness of Earth feels you here. Your vibrational frequency is felt by animals and all life on this planet. The Light that you carry within is your power. You are the Light of the world. Everything is part of the One Expression of Source. We are the creation of Supreme Divine Essence. You are the Light of the Divine among humanity. Your essence is needed here on the Earth. You emit high frequencies felt throughout this galaxy and beyond. When life gets overwhelming, know that you are on assignment and you will return to your home of origin that matches this powerful Light. Never forget your importance.

You are being prepared to be a Master Soul and offered spiritual employment. We are destined to become colleagues of the One Loving Source. There are positions to be filled—spiritual positions.

It is really unfortunate that most people only keep company with their ego, when their Soul is wanting their attention. Choose Soul over the egoic mind. Say out loud, "I am Soul." When making this statement, who is the "I" stating this? When making this statement, it is the Soul talking to the ego/mind. You are a Divine Soul and don't let your ego tell you differently. One you start identifying with your true identity as a Soul, you raise yourself above the human consciousness. You see things differently now and are not subject to only the ego's viewpoint. In the beginning of a deep spiritual path, the outer is reality and the inner is a dream; however, further along down the path, it flips so the outer is the Waking Dream and the inner is the true reality. Ask any person who has gone through a Near Death Experience (NDE) and they will wholeheartedly state that the other side is a higher reality and more real. How one views the world in the I AM state is completely different from when they were keeping company with their ego/mind. A person will walk the earth very differently and view themself and the world with an ever-expanding consciousness, and the Soul is on the path toward Self-Realization and God Realization attainment. Once a person steps into the I AM consciousness, they can see the antics of the ego so easily and can keep it in check. Sometimes they can even laugh about how the ego views things.

The purpose of life is Self-Realization and God Realization. What is more important than your connection and identity with the Supreme Infinite Source?

You are already Self-Realized. You are already God-Realized. You need to disassociate from your ego aspect of your mind. Staying in the human consciousness is hindering your spiritual ascent. A true spiritual path is about remembering your true identity as a Soul who is a piece of Source. The Divine Presence is within you and is you. You just don't believe it. As you spend more time on a consciousness-expanding path, you will come to realize this truth.

The only way to move from service to self is to merge your personal will with the Divine Will. This frees your Soul from the bondage of the physical senses and the outside world to service to the Divine Plan. You are a spark of the Infinite Light, a piece of the Divine Essence. When a person comes to remember their true identity, an awakening takes place. Soul remembers and is unable to allow the ego to be in control anymore. This is a revolutionary shift in consciousness to Oneness and a higher call to service. Service to Source is service to all life.

The head and the heart must come together if a person is going to get beyond the human consciousness.

We need to be self-aware. Another way of putting it is shadow work: the ability to see how our actions, behaviors, and triggers affect all the people around us. Then we need to do the necessary work to perform self-evaluation to elevate our human interactions to reflect a friendly attitude.

You don't have to be the perfect spiritual student. Do your best each day and keep moving forward, even if it is only a small step.

Bring your awareness that you have gained into all your dealings in your life. Self-analysis is part of a spiritual path. Practice being watchful of your ego, personality, and emotions ruling you. Allow the Higher Self to be your guide and in control to keep things in perspective.

The spiritual evolution of human consciousness up to Self-Realization and God Realization is the divine science of the most sacred.

To the mind and ego, walking the path is difficult. To the Soul, it is easy and enjoyable.

Everyone is focusing on something, from the ordinary to the highly esoteric. What are you remembering? What is on your mind? Yes, do your daily duties, yet remember that you are a Divine Being in a physical form experiencing a human journey. Remember that you are a Soul on Earth as you go through your day. This will change your whole perspective on how you walk through life. The goal of a true spiritual teacher is to remind the students of their true identity. It is the ego that performs the identity theft. A Master Soul never allows the student to become dependent on the teacher. A true spiritual teacher instructs the student to become a Master Soul in their own right.

At some point in your spiritual journey, you will need to sacrifice everything. It is called your Ego Self. When you get to the level where you can see it in action, really see it, then the Ego knows it's on the radar. The Ego can't hide anymore. Even when you have befriended your Ego, you still have to keep a watchful eye on it. It is tricky in the beginning on a profound spiritual path. The Ego can cause all sorts of problems to keep you off the path or while you are on the path, for it does not want to be found out, much less controlled. The enemy on your transcendental path is your Ego. This is a separate entity that can be your worst opponent. Ancient yogis have mentioned the power of the Ego and how it is an appendage to the Soul in order to navigate a physical reality. When you are asleep, it helps you, yet when you become spiritually awakened, then it does not want to step aside and let the Soul rule all aspects of your life. This is why all high-level spiritual teachers will tell you that there is a sacrifice that needs to be paid. The Ego does not get eliminated; it gets tamed and calmed. At first the seeker feels the sacrifice is too much yet comes to realize that is the ultimate freedom. Being free from the antics of your Ego is the highest freedom you can experience in physical form. When I mean being free, you can always see the Ego. You will know when it is stepping on the toes of your Soul and trying to push the Soul off the throne. Even after you have reached your spiritual attainments, you have to keep an eye on the Ego, for it knows when it is not being watched. Stay connected to your Higher Self so you can stay in control. Otherwise, your Ego will be running your life and not you, your Higher Self, your Soul.

The shadow part of your Ego is the one that gets extremely angry and shows obsessive greed, vanity, severe lust, and excessive attachment. When dealing with this aspect of your Ego, you must be very careful and convincing. Use love and persuasion in order to get this under control. You cannot use force, for it will bite you horribly in order to stay alive; therefore, you have to proceed gently. You can't enter into the higher realms without doing your shadow work. What is shadow work? Self-analysis and self-awareness of how you affect the people all around you—your behaviors, your judgments, your thoughts toward others, your emotional outbursts, your actions and dealings with others, your inner dialogue, and so on.

Life will have its ups and downs. On a spiritual path, you are not expected to be perfect. Only your best efforts are required.

Never Back Down! You can take a break when you need to, then move forward. The adversary will try to conquer you with every thought, emotion, and outer situation. Light Workers, hold your ground. This is what you came here for, and the mass awakening is now happening on this planet. The mass awakening is talked about on all the social media sites. We need to get into our positions for this significant assignment. Lock in your powerful light. You came to Earth for this, and you have power. It is within you. You have the power of Source, for you are created from Source; thereupon, it is your true essence. You are a Higher Light Being, an angel of a spiritual war that is taking place on the Earth at this time. There is no place where Source is not. Source is all of us together. Source is not separate from us. Source pervades everything. It is just the Ego that has been distorted by being in a lower plane of existence and forced to live in a corrupt world system. We have corruption on all levels, and now the Light Workers are waking up and remembering their assignments. The darkness is going to be cleared away due to the high-frequency light that is now coming to this planet, and the Light Workers are the boots on the ground who are among humanity. Light Workers, keep your eye on the goal and your purpose work. Don't get too lost in the details of life. Can you see beyond your own life existence? Humanity needs you. Be unbreakable. Shine Your Light Brightly. You beam like the stars. You are a Massive Powerful Divine Being. Never forget this! Yes, you are a human being temporarily; just don't get lost in it. You have just forgotten where you came from before you incarnated to Earth and your power. When this assignment is completed, your human life, you will return back Home. It is like walking off a battlefield where you were victorious. Nothing is wasted in this life. Your battle scars show your service to the Divine Plan. When you cross over the veil and transition from this physical life, you will see much more fully. In order to be a general, you have to experience the battlefield. The Earth University is an extremely high level of training and experience. You are on a Spiritual Special Forces assignment. This is your journey to glory. See what you have become on this human journey. Light Worker, yell your battle cry, pick up your sword, and pierce the darkness. Your mighty infinite light is more powerful than any darkness. Yes, this is a dark world, but that is why you came here. Know you are one of many here on this mission. Let the Love of Source sustain you. Find a community of others who are awake and who remember their call to come to Earth and bring light to it. Since you are made of the One Source, you are a god in human form. Hold your head high, for you are a powerful Divine Being. You also came here to understand this. You had to step away temporarily from what you knew to understand more fully who you are and your power. You are gods of light from the Supreme Infinite Light. Never Back Down from the spiritual battle. You have got this, regardless of appearances.

In time, the mind/ego will enjoy the path. The spiritual journey is not to eliminate the ego. It is about retrieving the throne from the ego and rightfully adorning the true royalty, the Soul. On a high spiritual path, you are trying to love something greater than your ego and personality.

The Ego is like a spoiled child. It wants everything and does not care how it gets it, whom it hurts, and so forth. You will feel you are always disciplining it constantly and gradually. Sometimes you will need to use love, and other times you will need to use instruction. You cannot discipline the Ego too harshly, for it will become rebellious. If you use too much love, the Ego will play with you and still do what it wants, so you can't be too soft on it. Moderation and balance are required. You will come to know which side is needed depending upon the situation. Connect to your Higher Self and ask what is needed. This is why it is important to develop this inner connection and dialogue. This path can be treacherous, and this is why spiritual students will look for a guide, a mentor, or a teacher who has experience on this journey. When you are on a quest, it is advisable to have a skilled guide to help you navigate the pitfalls. I even had Master Soul Teachers when I was working on my spiritual attainments. Some of them were tough, but they were also strong and powerful. Some of my teachers were soft and approachable, yet their love was very needed and effective as well. Life will test us to see how well we are doing.

Nothing is lost or wasted. Breathe Deeply. Can you feel the Love that is Within you? Your heart beating and the flow of your tears. You can find love in your pain and sorrow. You can find love even when you are alone and need to find the strength to carry on. Your love can comfort others. You are never alone; it just appears this way while in a physical form. When you feel disconnected, this agony will lead you to go Within. This is where the peace that surpasses all understanding can be found and experienced. This is the place to feel the greatest love and for you to reconnect with your Soul. No one or any object can take the place of this sacred connection with your Soul. If you are here, then you have a great purpose. You are on the journey of Soul. Never give up when it grows dark. Stay connected and go within for the Divine Guidance. You have it always with you and carry it Within. You are deeply loved and needed.

Psychic forces prey upon people. When you get extremely angry, don't you feel something has been chewing on you? Awareness is vital to keep you from being preyed upon. Psychic entities look for low-vibrational people because their energy field around them is very thin and weak. Keep your vibrational frequency as high as possible to stay safe and protected. Highly evolved people are distasteful to psychic beings in the psychic realities that influence us in deceptive ways. Call on your Higher Self when you are in trouble for help to get out of these extreme emotions, thoughts, and actions. I cannot stress enough how awareness is your protection; stay as best you can in a high-vibrational frequency. Put on music that inspires you. Go outside into nature, go take a bike ride, look at what is going on around you and evaluate the situation. Awareness is your superpower.

A spiritual standard is loving Source, loving the creation, and loving being in service to the Divine Plan.

You can't fix a state of consciousness. Anger is still going to stay the same and be anger each time you go to that vibrational level. You have to rise above the vibrational level of anger. Greed and vanity are never going to disappear, for if you visit that vibrational level of greed or vanity, you will experience it. You cannot change these aspects of the mind. You need to learn how to transcend them by raising your consciousness instead of trying to fix or modify them.

If the world rejects you, then don't be dismayed. You are in good company, my friend, for many great Master Soul Teachers were rejected, and some of them were killed because the public was too low vibrationally to appreciate them. Your greatest love is Within. Most Master Souls don't care for the world and are interested only in helping sincere students get to the highest spiritual level possible. Otherwise, they spend time doing spiritual work, such as writing, going inward, spending time in nature, and so on. Master Souls do have daily duties, yet even when they are performing them, their mind is on the Divine Presence.

Detachment is not something you do on the outer; it is something you do on the inner. What is the inner reality that is playing inside your mind? The past? A worry? A highly charged emotion? Do what you need to do to resolve the issue, then surrender it over for the Divine Will and then detach. The next step is to focus on what you want to experience, not what you don't want. You succeed at detachment by elevating your consciousness and becoming attached to something higher, which is the Divine Presence.

There will be a lot of things you will not be able to fully understand until you rise to Self-Realization and God Realization. Children don't understand adulthood with all the responsibilities until they reach adulthood themselves.

What makes the path intense is staying awake and aware constantly. The students who live the spiritual life as best as they can shift into higher states of consciousness more quickly. It is very simple and deals with what you want. What vibrational state do you want to spend your day in? A high or low level of consciousness?

When you first get up in the morning, you need to remember that you are a Divine Being in a physical form having a human experience. Feel the Divine Presence Within you. Your Soul is a piece of Source, and that is what makes you immortal, eternal, and infinite. Let the love from your Soul come in and let yourself get filled with this power. You are love in physical form. Fall in love with your Soul Self.

Do you want to have a happy day? Stay close to your Higher Self. Part of the journey is getting to know who you are and who you are not.

Most students starting the path love their ego and personality more than their Soul. I know this may surprise many people. Prior to realization, seekers are submerged into the world of appearances. Over time on the path, the ego starts to diminish. Over time the student develops a relationship with their indwelling Soul Self. A Master Soul Teacher will enlighten you and reveal spiritual truths through their writings. Upon reading them, the seeker sees the teachings as elevated and esoteric. Learning the wisdoms allows the student to leave the body consciousness and shift into higher levels of consciousness.

The purpose of being on a spiritual path is to be awakened to your true identity, to achieve your attainments, which are your spiritual goals and your purpose work on Earth. We end up transcending from our Lower Self (Personal Will) to our Higher Self (Divine Will) and perform service to the Divine Plan. Some people feel they are down here only to have a good time. We are in spiritual school and on assignment, although the playground captures most attentions. Yes, we can play, yet let us not be consumed by it and believe that it is the only reason for a human incarnation.

Spiritual death has nothing to do with a physical death. Master spiritual teachers are talking about the death of the Ego and personality, which really entails the purification of both. A purified Ego is not running your life, for it allows for the Soul Self to be in control and wearing the crown. Redirection of spiritual currents of our energy toward higher levels of consciousness—this is the divine purpose for your spiritual unfoldment. When pains of separation are discussed, this is a stage along the path of spiritual evolution. This stage can be so intense that it can consume the person. The outward experience is the tears that come uncontrollably because their heart has been pierced so profoundly. The spontaneous tears are shed to put out the intensity of their longing for union with the Divine. The tears help extinguish the fire of the pains of separation. This is a stage to purify and prepare someone for reaching higher-vibrational frequencies. This level causes replacement of the ego with the Divine Essence. The intense tears of longing can happen in the stage of the Union or in the stage of the Bliss. Many times, it can happen in both stages. The sacred journey takes place in four stages, and the Four Stages are listed in the final pages of this book. One's love becomes a fire in this ecstatic state as the Soul is enraptured by the Divine Love. The mystical experiences in this stage cause absorption with the Divine Source. This is love of the purest form. These spontaneous tears are uncontrollable. They just flow, and the water helps with the intensity of this stage on the sacred mystical journey.

A Master Soul Teacher will explain, write books, and give classes and retreats, yet what the teacher is trying to do is get you into the water. You can learn how to swim only when you finally get into the water. This path is experiential. Yes, you need instruction, and you need to learn information; however, the teacher knows that eventually the student needs to get into the water to experience swimming. The mind can take you only so far, and then it has to step aside so the Soul can take over and get into these higher levels that are beyond duality and the mental planes of existence. In their guidance, the Master Soul knows what you are going to need to do and knows this is an uphill journey. Spiritual attainments are a very high accomplishment and can take many years. It is like climbing a mountain. Take breaks when you need to and then continue forward. When you get to the top, then you will say it was worth the time and effort. The view from the top of the mountain will change your perspective permanently. The Master Soul Teacher is not the one who hands out the attainments. You receive Self-Realization and God Realization when your vibrational frequency reaches a certain level that equals that attainment. That is how it works. The teacher is the guide and mentor on this path with you, for they themselves have spent years and sometimes their entire lives working on these attainments. Master Souls have reached Mastery Level and therefore have been asked to help other Souls who are ready for this path. There is no doctrine, no philosophy, no beliefs, because the spiritual attainments are beyond all those teachings. It deals with Mastery of all three levels in your cosmology, which are the Physical Plane, the Emotional Plane, and the Mental Plane. Mastery of these levels is for the sincere student. If you want mastery of these three levels, then your homework is waiting for you. If you want freedom from the ego controlling you and your life, then this path will help you get beyond and allow your Soul to rule in your life. Master Souls are not any more special than any other Soul. They just got an earlier start, are further along, and are here in service. Master Souls know that eventually the students will reach mastery. How quickly depends upon the effort put forth, sincerity, and receptivity.

The spiritual journey is to transfer from states of consciousness to the Oneness of the I AM pure consciousness.

There is no end to the expansion of your consciousness. You will spend eternity expanding and acting in service to Source's Divine Plan. Your love for the Supreme Essence will be so great that you will spend eternity being in service. The higher one goes, the more they serve with great love to the Divine Plan. We are talking about true Mastership and Divine Connection.

As you continue on the spiritual path, you will unfold, your consciousness will expand, and you will start to have spiritual experiences. The Ego slides to the side, and these mystical experiences are beyond the mind and ego. Be patient, for in time you will have your own spiritual experiences. Continue with each step daily toward spiritual advancement. This is all part of the unfoldment process.

Heaven are hell are not places. They are states of consciousness. I am sure that you have experienced heaven and hell right within you, and then there is an outward manifestation of what is taking place inside. If your thoughts are torturing you, then that is a form of hell right there. People think they have to translate in order to get to heaven. When you leave your physical form, you go to the vibrational level you have achieved in consciousness. There are untold levels on the other side—dimensions upon dimensions, all based upon vibrational frequencies. Why do you think so many Souls on Earth are working on expansion of their consciousness and attainment of spiritual goals? They understand this spiritual energetic law of vibrational frequencies. If you want to hang out and reside at the vibrational level with Master Souls and supreme Hierarchs, then I suggest sorting out what is really important to you: something you can carry beyond this life when you translate. Everything stays behind except your spiritual accomplishments. We are all in the Cosmic University and moving up through the levels. There have been many extremely high-level Souls who have incarnated on this planet. We all have to pull rotation for the lower grades. We are in service to help our fellow brother and sister Souls. We came here to help those who got lost along the journey. We came here to help others wake up from the Waking Dream. The fog, the veil, it wipes our memory when we cross into the physical dimension. Our intense light and vibrational frequency are causing a mass awakening now taking place on this planet. Many of you reading this book are highly evolved and master-level Souls who are on assignment here. You recognize the vibrational frequency of this book and were attracted to it, and here it is in your hands. Creating this book was an assignment asked of me and is one among many acts of service I lovingly perform for the Divine Plan.

As one ascends, the heart is filled with endless love; the difficult part is trying to absorb all the divine ecstasy and bliss. This causes a willingness to incarnate into the physical dimension in service to other Souls. Some of you are saying you didn't expect for it to be this hard being in the third-dimensional level. The third dimension is low, dense, and dark. Many of you remember where you came from prior to incarnation, and this third dimension is extremely painful due to the ruthless and merciless vibrational states here. All Master Souls have not expressed kind words about this dimension. Level three is a low level. Just look at the news and see how the unawake Souls treat each other. According to mainstream society, highly evolved

Souls are not usually accepted or appreciated. I am still shocked at what goes on down here. You holding this book means you are an advanced Soul. Most people are not interested in spiritual advancement. I am here to remind you of what you already know. This is about you remembering your true identity as a Divine Being, your power, your purpose work, and your sacred connection to Source. Many supreme Hierarchs call Source the Divine Love Frequency.

Why would Source send us to this dark, low third dimension? An entire-day retreat could be spent talking about this question. In short, there are a number of reasons, not just one. Life is not that simple. However, I will provide an example. Parents send their children off to school. They know there will be painful, frustrating, and joyful experiences, yet what the children learn in school is of great value. Even the schoolteachers can get tired, yet they continue with their roles and responsibilities. The Earth School has enrolled students and teachers at all levels. Some Souls are in grade school, and others are at the university level achieving mastery. All grade levels are open at the Earth School. If you are reading this book, then you are at a level to work on Mastership. Regardless of how this book ended up in your hands, it means you have been asking the advanced questions. You have been seeking and wanting to know more.

We have many Master Souls on this planet at this time. Not all Master Souls are teaching, nor are they teachers. Some come here to have their high vibration on this planet. My original and main assignment for coming here was to be an energetic administer in service. Then I was asked to write so that the spiritual wisdoms and attainments could be accessible to the public and would be available to teach and further discuss.

Can you step in and dance to the symphony of music from the Supreme Source Conductor? Step into your cosmic power and be the dance partner with the Beloved.

If you are going to try to walk the entire spiritual path by your mind, it won't work. The mind can take you only so far. Your mind won't be able to handle the difficulties on the spiritual journey on its own. This path takes you beyond your ego, so how is it going to help you when you have reached that point on your spiritual journey? There is a level where the mind has to step aside and only the Soul can go forward. Why? Because the spiritual journey to Self-Realization and God Realization is beyond the mind/mental realms. Mental powers don't operate in the higher celestial realms. The mind is dual in nature. Non-duality realms are above the mind power. This is why many spiritual students plateau. They can't figure it out with their mental power. The path of Self-Realization and God Realization attainment is a path where you surrender your ego/mind complex in order to get beyond it, because the mind can't take you there. It is a path of being intoxicated by the love of Infinite Source, union, Oneness, bliss, absorption, and freedom. On this path, you will be giving up your egoic mind step by step along the way.

The complete surrender and commitment come when you have attained God Realization. You can't surrender all at once or give everything up that you previously claimed as your identity, which is your ego/mind complex. Once God Realization attainment has occurred, your whole identity has repositioned, and then your level of service is total commitment to Source's Divine Plan. Many of you are already God-Realized, yet you need to wake up and remember that you came down here on assignment and already are in service to the Divine Plan. You cannot do anything other than serve Source, for you have experienced Oneness with Source. It is hard to even put into words. This level of surrender can come only with an identity shift in consciousness. God Realization is a marvelous goal, for it will transform your consciousness completely. Then you will be given new assignments.

The mind thinks spirituality is right and wrong and is concerned about the morality of good and bad. The mind is dual in nature so will never see shades of gray. There are many situations that do not fit the morality code of good and bad. True spirituality does not deal with the intellectual standards of the dualistic mind. The highest level of spirituality deals with living a true spiritual life where the person doesn't just walk the path; they become the path. The path is within you, hence the oneness with the path.

Spiritual Mastership deals with living in a higher consciousness level of Oneness, unity, and service to others, to name a few.

Our consciousness will fluctuate moment to moment, for energy is always moving through us. This is mental energy, emotional energy, and physical energy that flow through each person. You will have higher or lower energetic movement, and then when you get back to the center, you reside in your overall vibrational level. Where you spend most of your day vibrationally is your stasis and harmony.

The Master Souls will clearly state that if anything is not eternal and cannot last beyond the physical dimension, it is temporary. All that you experience in this dimension can exist only for a fleeting period of time. When you cross the veil and leave this physical existence, what can you take with you? Your spiritual advancements can cross the veil, for they are eternal and of a higher frequency than the mental, emotional, and physical.

If Self-Realization is your goal, then the ego cannot remain in the primary position. The Soul can escape from the control of the ego only when it has experienced seeing itself in pure form without the body, ego, personality, and shadow self. All is removed, and only the pure energetic essence is seen during the mystical experience of Self-Realization. Nothing compares to seeing your true identity as the energetic sovereignty of your Soul. Someone can tell you, yet it is not until you have a direct experience that you know. You are classified as a Knower of your true identity. Self-Realization is realization of your True Self. Once you experience Self-Realization, you can never go back to your old identity. You are forever transformed and liberated from the confines of your ego/mind complex. You still have these appendages to serve you while you are here in physical form; however, your True Self is ruling your universe.

A spiritual student needs to come to the awareness that the Infinite Source Creator is present Within them. The Soul is spiritual royalty. This is hidden yet needs to be discovered. Before you can be realized in Self and God attainment, you need to know of your divinity.

A spiritual student's goal is not only to attain God Realization but also to accept a spiritual assignment. All highly evolved Souls are given a mission prior to incarnating, yet when they get down here, they forget and get lost in the circus of life. It is to be expected in the beginning, for one needs to adjust down here and experience life in the third-dimensional field. Then there comes a time for them to awaken and remember their goals and purpose work. Even when they remember their assignment, some Souls will feel uncomfortable or overwhelmed because they feel the heavy responsibility of what will be asked of them. These Souls need encouragement to step out and start serving the Divine

Will instead of their personal will. Many of you are Starseeds from higher realms. You came here for service. You must become adept, just like the other Master Souls who have come before on this planet. This is what is being offered to you when you attain God Realization. There are plenty of spiritual positions that need to be filled in service to the Divine Plan, which is the grand overall design for this universe.

All paths ultimately lead a person to the path of Self-Realization and God Realization. It may take several lifetimes, yet when they are ready, the path will be exposed to them. All paths are needed and are the stepping-stones for an evolving consciousness. This is similar to the 12 grades in the educational system.

In the Earth School, every Soul is learning at different levels. Some are at grade-school level, and others are in university training. Master Soul instructors will teach the Souls who are ready to evolve their consciousness. The ultimate goal is for a spiritual student to reach Mastership level. Some students who have reached their attainments will teach; however, many will be handed other spiritual assignments. The spiritual assignments come from the higher realms. Master Souls know there need to be replacements, for they won't be on the planet. Soul's attainment is service at a higher level showing the Divine Reality within and Soul's reason for existence. It is appropriate validation to be fully qualified, which leads into a deeper level of service to Source's Divine Plan.

It is important to think for yourself. Do your research first, then make your own decision. Everyone has a different experience that they will draw from; however, use your own experience to draw your final decision on people and situations. Mass media tries to influence people in one direction or another. Keep your individuality and be careful of conformity.

If you can't take it with you when you leave your physical form, then the value is low regardless of appearances. Enjoy your items and your physical life, for they provide your lessons, tests, experiences, and selfless service.

Are you feeling homesickness? This feeling is inherent in the Soul when it comes from Source. There is nothing wrong with what you are feeling. You are away from your home of origin. Soul has a long journey in the lower planes of existence for training and Divine service.

Many people are experiencing an identity crisis. The population identifies with their nationalism, race, religious belief, political party, educational degrees, fashion, profession, hobbies, and other outside activities. They are none of these, only a temporary appearance casting an illusion of their true identity. They are identifying with the mental inner and outer capacities, not the True Self, the Soul. When they are trapped in their mental states, this can bring depression, anxiety, fear, and misery. The Soul is none of these mental states and wants to identify with its true essence of Source.

You are a Soul and not a temporary state of consciousness that you experience as an emotion, a thought, or a physical action. Soul needs to have a wide range of experiences. You need to understand that there is a huge difference between a state of consciousness and consciousness itself as the I AM consciousness.

We are multidimensional beings. When you are thinking about something, you are in your mind. When in your emotions, you are feeling the sadness or the joy. When in the physical form, you will feel physical sensations. When you are in your Soul Self, you will be the observer and will see all aspects of your Lower Self with all the performances.

Once someone receives the spiritual bliss of Divine Love, nothing else matters. This love is so powerful that the Soul wants to stay in absorption of the Divine Presence that is within them. It does not mean that they don't live in the outside world; they recognize that the inner is more real than the outer because they have traveled their realms within and know the difference between the two.

Self-Realization and God Realization do not mean you have freedom from all the difficulties; however, they do provide the ability to transcend them, for you see these as temporary circumstances.

Let people live out their lives and allow things to run their course. You cannot change another person. Only they can change themselves, and they have to do their own inner work. Be happy that your awareness is high enough to see the value in expanding your consciousness. As best as you can, stay close to the Divine Presence and know that this power is Within you.

A Realized Soul cares little for the world and the ego/mind complex. They will play their role and complete their assigned mission. The Realized Soul is always ready to go to their home of origin, back to where they resided prior to this physical incarnation. Every day they remember they are on assignment. They have no attachment to this world, for they know it is very temporary. Realized Souls accomplish their assignments to the best of their abilities. Master Souls look forward to the day they get to translate and leave the physical dimension, for they remember their Family of Light and cannot wait to be reunited with them.

They have fulfilled their service to the Divine Plan in this dimension and continue to serve on other future assignments. Some days can be hard for them here since they remember and sometimes visit while sleeping in the dimensional level that they came from prior to accepting this assignment on Earth.

The love needs to increase in the spiritual student. All spiritual victories are won through the power of love. When given a choice between power versus force, power always wins. Love is the highest power. Sometimes love is strong, and sometimes it is tender. Soul knows what type of love is needed for each situation.

When Souls get tired of the circus of life, they start to look for a spiritual teacher who can help them reunite with the Oneness and their Family of Light. Talk about a celebration—you cannot imagine it until you have experienced it directly. There is this enormously vast celebration, and everyone from the dimensional level that they came from receives this excitement of reuniting, and the love flows along with music you have never heard on Earth before. Sheer bliss is experienced when a Soul gets back home. Then you are Realized, and when you come back down to Earth to complete your assignment, the physical dimension seems so dull in comparison. This is why Realized Souls don't care for this world much and spend time connecting to a higher reality. They perform their daily duties and purpose work, yet their hearts are attached to the Divine Presence within them.

The wise spiritual student realizes that the mind cannot deliver the complete, utter happiness that they desire. A person has to go to a higher realm beyond the mental powers of the mental dimensions.

You are welcome to stay down in the lower dimensions until you get tired of all the circus rides. After a while the Soul wants to return home. In the end, you decide when you are ready for the evolutionary journey toward realization and your home of origin.

When you feel loneliness, your Soul is homesick, yet the mind perceives it as though you need outward company.

When you lie down at night to sleep, the body needs to rest, yet Soul never sleeps. Many nights are journeys into other dimensions. The reason you don't remember them is that you are visiting realms beyond the mind, the subconscious, and the mental dimensions. This is why sometimes you wake up more tired in the morning than when you went to sleep. Many times, upon waking in the morning, if a person or pet who has passed from the physical world comes to your consciousness, you very well could have been with them that night while your body was resting. Your consciousness is nonlocal, for it can be everywhere simultaneously. Your Soul is a piece of Source and therefore has the power of being omnipresent. This being present in all places at all times offers the ability for night travels. The Soul requires experiences for expansion. No matter where one is on the Divine Journey of Soul, the experiences in many dimensions are necessary.

The Ego feels it can do a better job of providing happiness to the spiritual student than the indwelling Soul. Each seeker needs to choose between their ego and a higher reality. This choice happens to all spiritual students. Each person has to deal with their Ego, which stands in the way of spiritual realization. The student comes to realize that only the Soul can provide real happiness.

Your Soul has supreme power over your ego/mind complex.

The spiritual seeker is a rare individual of an exceptional level of consciousness uncommon to the general population. These Souls are remarkable in their quest for upward movement in consciousness. Once a person reaches the seeker level, they desire to realize that their life needs to be more than being centered around their ego and personality. Spiritual students realize that they are Divine Beings. They are eager for spiritual truths that answer the mystery of life. They have a sense of knowing that there are spiritual wisdoms out there. There is a deep longing that causes the seeker to start the search. Further along on the path, there are pains of separation. The path eventually brings them to the attainments of Self-Realization and God Realization. At some point, the seeker realizes the spiritual journey is about spiritual truths. Once the seeker moves into the stage of surrender, they start to focus on yielding their personal will to the Divine Will for their life. They will focus on a spiritual life and service to the Divine Plan. As the student is impacted by the path, they will naturally be attracted to the next stage, called the Union. The following stage is called the Bliss. Please see the Four Spiritual Stages that are listed in the final pages of this book.

Source is constantly creating new universes; therefore, we will never equal the Infinite Essence that pervades all.

Remember: there is no shadow without the Light.

Until the ego/mind complex is spiritualized, it can be antagonistic toward the indwelling Soul. A spiritual teacher helps to uncover and reveal the processes and traps that are set by the ego to stay in total control. Spiritual students who are on a path to become Realized Souls are rare in the population, for these individuals see the highly coveted attainments as having significant worth. Allowing the Soul to awaken, enabling the spiritual power to control the ego/mind complex, is a great treasure to people who realize that the attainment of spiritual goals offers spiritual potential and mastery.

A true path will help you differentiate between truth and illusion, what is absolute truth and relative truth, Soul and mind, Divine Will and your own personal will.

There is no place that the Divine Essence is not. Therefore, you can see that time and matter are an illusion. There is nowhere to go, and there is no distance to travel in order to come in contact with the Omnipresent Source.

You have to put on your armor each day, for the adversary is an energy that all the past Master Souls have discussed, and awareness is important.

Spirituality is to elevate from the human consciousness to a more transcendental and spiritual consciousness. The population varies in spiritual interest. Currently, there is large interest for spiritual progress on the Earth. Individuals are looking for deeper meaning in their lives, and very little seems to satisfy them anymore. As people get older and they begin to face their own mortality, they start to feel they need direction in their course of spiritual evolution. Then the big questions start to appear, causing motivation for the seeker to start their quest for spiritual truths. A Master Soul has such compassion for the human condition. Most Souls don't even know about their Divine nature, much less how to navigate the ego/mind complex. Most individuals don't know when they are in their ego or connecting with the Higher Self. Spiritual mastery is similar to a child becoming an adult. It is an exploration, and many experiences occur before adulthood is reached. A spiritual journey will take time, effort, and growing experiences. Spiritual Mastership will require ardent training. Most people feel their ego and personality are their identity and have no idea that this is temporary. The seeker does not understand how to distinguish between the Soul and the mind, their inner dimensions, and the awareness of illusory conditions.

Desire Mastership! You want to be a Master of your own cosmology of thoughts, emotions, imprints from the subconscious, and actions.

Most belief systems do not know the difference between the Soul and the ego/mind complex. The two realities within the human are the ego/mind/personality complex and the Soul. In the beginning of the spiritual journey of a mystical path, there is a conflict. The ego wants to stay in control, and the Soul awakens to realize its divinity, the Higher Self. The Higher Self can cause situations to occur for the true identity to finally emerge, offering spiritual authority in a person's life. A person's spiritual guides and angelic helpers will look for the highest-vibrational spiritual teacher for help with the level of Mastership.

We can get caught up in life's responsibilities. The egoic mind is required to handle all these situations. However, if we can take a moment and a deep breath, we will see that there is a higher perspective of the overall objective and course of this life.

The descent downward into the lower dimensions is called devolution. When the Soul is on the way upward toward the higher realms, it is called evolution. One of the purposes of life is to realize your divine identity and to gain many experiences along the way.

Make peace with your life.

The mind relies on the energy of the Soul. The mind does not provide the life force for the human body or the mind. When the Soul leaves the human, the form is lifeless, and the conscious mind stops functioning. It is the luminous Soul who is the generating power. Notice how you never have to plug in your human body to any outside power source. Since the Soul is a part of the Infinite Power Source, it is the eternal flame with the energetic light of the supreme majestic sound frequency.

A Master Soul will teach a student to know real from unreal.

You can become a Spiritual Master in this life. It is available to you and can be achieved. It is the highest ideal in human form.

Your Soul can experience the rarified higher states of consciousness. There is a path that offers this ability to experience the all-pervading, eternal, nameless, formless, limitless, everlasting, majestic, permanent, glorious, and celestial essence that is within you. This is why the human body is also called the human temple. If you only knew your own essence—and you have the opportunity to experience your true identity as a piece of Source while you are living in this physical form. An advanced spiritual path will liberate you from the controlling effects of the mind, which is the barrier that is in the way of freedom and you becoming a Master Soul in your own divine right. When an individual is ready, they will be attracted to start a spiritual journey into these divine mysteries. A natural affinity will be created between the student and the teacher. The Soul is the same essence as the Beloved Supreme Source. You end up falling in love with your own true identity and essence. Who is really calling you is the Beloved back home to be in union and remember? You have just forgotten—that's all—and I am reminding you of your divinity.

When a person says "I," they are referring to their ego/mind complex. "I went to the party." It was the ego mind and the physical body that went to the party. The Soul Self, the True Self, also called the I AM, is usually not identified as the one who is doing the outer activities. The Soul Self is the one who attains Self-Realization and God Realization. When a certain vibrational level is reached, Self-Realization and God Realization happen automatically and feel so natural.

The Soul is already pure, for it is a piece of Source, and therefore there is no difference between Soul and Source. The issue is there are coverings over the Soul, such as the mental body/thoughts, the astral/emotional body, and the physical body. These cause barriers for the Soul to have conscious union with the Divine Presence within. We have the connection, yet the coverings cause constraints, making people feel there is separation.

The negative force in the human body is the ego. The positive power in the human body is the Soul. The spiritual battle is that both are trying to be in control. Do not be concerned, for the Soul will win, providing sound guidance on your human journey.

The True Self is really what an individual wants to meet. Seeing the actual Soul Essence becomes the quest to know who we really are when all the coverings are removed. Realization of the True Self is Self-Realization of our Divinity. The Soul does not rise to the surface beyond the coverings of the physical, emotional, and mental without the ego aspect of the mind causing a struggle to keep control. When a person is on a spiritual path that challenges the ego, it can be a spiritual battle. The mind will fight the Soul. Eventually, the egoic mind will become spiritualized, tame, and in harmony with the Soul. This is when the surrender of the ego comes and serves the Soul. The raising of the student's energies causes this awakening and purification process of the ego, emotions, personality, physicality, and shadow aspects of the mind. Once the Soul is in complete control over the mind's coverings, the body consciousness is transcended. The personal will serves the Divine Will.

Your true identity is within. Most people think their identity is in the outer world. Self-exploration is a significant part of the journey. An individual needs to know who they are first in order to understand who they are not. The stolen identity needs to be corrected. Their true identity is Soul. Their false identity is the ego. This is part of the enlightenment process. Becoming enlightened to the truth that we are all Divine Beings.

One of the goals is to know real from unreal. Soul is real, permanent, and infinite. Ego and personality are unreal, for they are aspects of the mind and are temporary. When a person leaves their physical form, the ego and personality that have been formed and utilized in this lifetime only stay connected to the time track for each particular incarnation. Divine Source and Soul are permanent and real because of their omnipresence, omnipotence, and omniscience. Since the Soul is made from Source, the infinite characteristic is the same. If anything is dual in nature or in distinction, it is the mind, thought waves, and mental powers. The Soul is beyond dimensions of duality. Soul is the generating power of the mind. The mind cannot function without the majestic power of the Soul, for it can exist on its own because it is a piece of Source.

Truth is eternal. Untruth is temporary and filled with illusion.

Identification with thought waves will cause a distortion of our identity. You are a Soul, and identification with anything else is unreal, meaning only temporary in this life. Once Self-Realization is attained, you no longer identify with the outer, unreal, and temporary world. You see that your true identity is energetic, beyond all the aspects of the mind. You have experienced being in a dimension beyond the mind and therefore have seen that you are not your mind and its mental powers. If you hang out with your mind all day, you will identify with the unreal and mistaken image of yourself. Remembering and staying with your true identity as a Soul keep you in the higher perspective in life.

The highest spiritual attainment to receive in physical form is Self-Realization and God Realization. It is a journey worth taking, for you as the Soul can be in control of the ego; have mastery of physical, emotional, and mental dimensions; and experience remembering your union with Source. No sacrifice, no Victory. Lightworkers, you are on assignment here to help humanity. You want to walk off the battlefield of this life in victory.

It is just a story, the reality of the senses. Acknowledge that it is a story and then you become the observer. Take your energy and attention back. This way you can stay with the Higher Self, the Soul. You are navigating Real from Unreal.

No one can take away what is in your destiny. Your Higher Self will give you everything.

Have firm faith. The worldly obligations you are fulfilling are all essentially spiritual. Everything is working in your favor regardless of appearances. Nothing is wasted, and all experiences are spiritual training. When you walk off the spiritual battlefield of your life, you are proud of all the battle scars you have accumulated in this lifetime.

Develop the inner dialogue with your Higher Self. Connect with this higher version of yourself throughout the day and grow this inner relationship. Know who is really by your side, because it comes from within, this vast power. Go through your day remembering you are a Divine Being and your connection with Source. Your consciousness will merge into that which you love. There is always love upon you as you go through your day. You just have to tap into it.

Grace is always there, for you will become strong. You have it already within you. Have no fear. We are connected as One, for we all come from the Great One Infinite Source.

Source is already in the saints and humanity. The only difference is that the ordinary person who is unawake has a veil of the ego that separates them from knowing their true identity of being a piece of Source. It is a concept until a person has the direct mystical experience of Self-Realization and God Realization. We are fortunate to have high-vibrational Souls on this planet. Humanity requires high-vibrational energy to counterbalance all the negativity in the human collective. The true reality is that we are all walking gods as Divine Beings. Most of humanity is interested only in career, family, children, wealth, status, and worldly affairs. Few are interested in seeing what is beyond the physical dimension. You just cannot imagine what you are dealing with and stay in constant connection with the highest power.

No matter what happens, always try to remain cheerful.

Source will be with you wherever you go.

Whatever is to happen has already happened. The Beloved will do whatever is for our benefit. No one can erase what is in your destiny. No one can have what is meant for you. Free Will also plays a role in your life. You will find that both destiny and Free Will cause you to have certain experiences.

Humanity does not enjoy any peace because it is not connected to Source on the outer consciously. On the inner we are connected, yet on the outer, we have forgotten the unity of how we are all One, for we are all made from the same Source. Humanity needs to be saved from the evils of egoism. A person can belong to any belief system and attain connection with the Divine Essence.

You do not have to give up your status or beliefs. Humanity can meet the Divine Presence within regardless of status or beliefs. Let us not get so attached to a Great Soul who lived thousands of years ago that we lose sight of the real reason for spirituality, which consists of the remembering of our true identity as Divine Beings and is the whole purpose of our human existence. The saints have taught that the Divine Source is within us. The present-day belief system teaches worship of the Great Souls of the past who have walked this planet, who actually taught us to love one another. The Divine Presence is beyond the mind and intellect. This is why we have to move beyond the lower dimensions of the physical, mental, and emotional planes to experience the Oneness and Realization of Self and God as existing within.

Many breaths are taken every day. Do not waste a breath. Remember that you are walking Divinity.

All Souls, no matter what country they may come from or what race they may belong to, are like flowers of different colors in the same garden. We are all living on the same planet and under the same sky. Dividing ourselves into groups, we have imprisoned ourselves in them. The Master Soul Teacher's objective is to free humanity from the cage of the egoic mind and body. Unfortunately, human consciousness has caused the bondage. All the different belief systems are getting the light from the same Supreme Candle. Why is there hostility between them? The whole point is to visit a temple or church and commune with the Divine. Today, religious centers have become commercial centers. The true value of the spiritual outcome has lost its hold. This is the reason the lovers of the Beloved remain distant from them. When people see hatred between the different belief systems, they question their whole purpose for existence. Why would any organization teach hostility toward others? This hatred between different groups of different types comes over hairsplitting distinctions made by ignorant persons who are themselves prey to selfishness, delusion, and pride. This engages them in cutting into pieces the unity of society. Their agenda is to push their own importance while usurping the rights of others. They are jealous of the praise or progress of anybody else. On the other hand, the Realized Souls are full of love for the Divine, and they have affection for all of creation. The real aim for all religions and political groups should be to teach and offer the same ethical and spiritual truths of unity for humanity, not division. Their work should unite humanity, not separate it

There is evolving and devolving of all species at all levels.

Set up the conditions in your life to have time daily to connect to your Higher Self. Remove the distractions and simply your life.

The world is a dream and only temporary. The mind is what causes the dream and wants it to continue. Purification of the

mind removes the veil, and then you can see the Oneness and Divine Essence.

You are so connected that you are hardwired to Source.

The Soul is hidden by many covers, such as the physical body, the mental body, and the emotional body. Moving beyond these covers is self-discovery, which is the essence of spirituality. The unity with the Divine cannot be comprehended by the mind and senses. Spirituality is knowing you are a Soul experiencing your inner regions and realizing the Divine with the Oneness together. Worldly knowledge is ignorant of the higher inner reality. The Divine pervades the whole universe, yet we cannot hear this Essence unless we withdraw from the outer noise and enter the inner silence. We do not have to give up our daily duties to follow an inner path. We can stay connected while performing our responsibilities. The stillness inside is always there, and we can just enter the stillness within whenever we like.

Through its own imagination, the mind creates self-deception.

Never follow the dictates of your own mind. Follow the wise guidance of your Soul Self.

You are a drop of Source. There is no you; there is only Source that pervades all and IS everything. This is about you coming to know who you are, which is a part of Source.

If you practice seeing the Beloved in the room, you will find that your conversation will always be of a spiritual nature.

Always remember that we do not belong to this world.

Humanity existed first, and all the religions and religious books came afterward. Various religions have come and gone, yet humans existed before any of them were established. Unless we know that we are Divine Beings, we are living in ignorance. If we try to know the Divine only through mental knowledge, we will be without spiritual experience. Take the path that will provide the inner spiritual experience, so we can directly see our inner dimensions and Divine Essence. It is one thing to be told and quite another to have a personal experience of it.

When you realize everything is Source, you entrust everything to the Beloved Supreme Essence. All becomes Source. You are also made of Source, a walking human temple, because of what is inside of you.

This world is the lowest and most miserable of all. As we go to higher realms, we enjoy more and more happiness. There is no peace in this world. Peace is with us, and we have to go beyond this physical dimension.

I gave up my life that I knew before, and now my life is no longer mine; it is the Beloved's to self-surrender. It is Thy Will Be Done now.

The Supreme Beloved has important plans for you. Let nothing sidetrack you. Keep love and harmony among yourselves. You are very useful in the hands of the Divine Presence in doing this very great work.

Do not worry about detachment. As you get into these higher-vibrational states of being, all the attachments fall away. This is not about mental acrobatics, where we use our mind to cause changes. Leave all that alone. Focus on achieving higher states of consciousness, and when you have arrived there, things will fall away naturally. You lose interest in them. You can still do them, yet you can take them or leave them. You will think, "I can go on a trip, or I can pass on the trip, yet I am fine either way." Many spiritual paths are into how you cannot do this or that. Focus on raising your frequency and being in these higher states of consciousness and this will cause situations to change on an energetic level in your inner and outer worlds. Some attachments will stay, and some will leave, according to what is the highest and best for you. Your Higher Self knows what is needed and not needed; therefore, trust this internal guidance within you.

There is a Homecoming Welcoming Banquet, and you are the guest of honor. Everyone in your dimension of origin is waiting for your return home.

When you think or say negative things, thought forms are created and hang around you.

You do not realize how important every minute is down here. Do not waste any time. Not a minute of this lifetime will be had again.

The Beloved is within you. People wander around and go to an outer temple or church while all along the true temple or church is within them. The unawake show respect to outer temples, while those of illuminated consciousness focus on adorning their heart and connection with the Divine Essence.

There is no greater wealth than progress on the spiritual path, a wealth that accompanies us even after death.

If you want to see the Beloved, do not cause grief to the heart of anyone. Source is never pleased with one who injures the feelings of others.

On a spiritual path that is based on spiritual love, the seeker comes to see that this is the life stream of this world and the essence of our lives. It is the very core of purity and simplicity. The Elixir of Love keeps life in full bloom. The spiritual student will go beyond their ego in order to drink from the cup of love. On the path of love, one has to be sincere in the quest of self-discovery and an inner relationship with the Supreme Beloved. The true lover is the Beloved. The Divine Presence becomes the Lover of such lovers. Spiritual love is such an intense intoxication that it takes us above the physical world and causes the inner mystical experience of being with the Beloved. Source is Love, and the Soul is made from Source. Love is a fire that burns away all evil tendencies from the egoic mind the moment it is awakened. The Beloved will say to you, "You are the only one in my eyes." When the Soul is touched by the Beloved, there is a constant flow of the stream of love.

No one is to believe a spiritual path blindly, for it can be experienced directly within the individual's own inner self.

True detachment consists of accepting the material comforts as well as the necessities of life merely to the extent of their usefulness for life, while realizing them to be only the means and not the goal. A truly detached person lives in this world but does not become entangled in it. The individual does not consider it necessary to leave the world in order to rise above it. They see the Presence of the Divine in everything. This individual lives in the world but is not attached to it.

You do not want to just read about spirituality. You want to experience spirituality.

The third-dimensional density provides valuable experience in a very important school and a test-drive for trillions of Souls. The Earth School provides the most extreme and toxic conditions to test, to get the experience, lessons, and information needed to continue evolution. In the third dimension, the density is so thick that it is suffocating. Many Souls came here from different Galaxies; they are known as the Starseeds. When they crossed the veil and entered into this incarnation on Earth, they lost their memory of the other dimensions and now are starting to awaken and remember their true identity and reason for coming here. How does an individual protect themselves against the low-vibrational frequencies in this third dimension? High spirituality is required to stay awake and aware in the Earth School. There are several large Absolute Cosmic Universities that send their students to Earth for ultimate testing and training. I compare it to spiritual Green Beret training for the next assignment in service to the Divine Plan. The lower the dimension, the greater the density, toxicity, hatred, greed, and cruelty and the more valuable experience the Soul can master.

You are in the process of becoming a saint. The saint sees the Creator everywhere. The saint sees life differently because their consciousness has been elevated and purified. You are on the path to sainthood. Start practicing this lifestyle. Live the spiritual life.

It is fortunate to hear of Self-Realization and God Realization attainments. It is rare that a person proceeds to pursue them. Then it is even rarer to achieve Self-Realization and God Realization, because they require tenacity. The path causes you to walk through difficult landscapes. When you are in love with the truth, then you are in love with the pathway to God through truth. This love causes the seeker to transcend the ego. Become friendly with your ego. You should see the ego as needing a friend to help it become agreeable with service to the Soul. Spirituality is really about overcoming selfishness and the conversion of the ego to be of service to your Higher Self. If you want to reach an advanced state of being, then you need to transcend the duality of either this or that or the us-against-them mentality. Duality causes separation. You want to dissolve the opposites. Spirituality is a new way of being in the world. This world is the grit that polishes you into a diamond. This world causes us to bring forth bravery, courage, stamina, determination, fortitude, endurance, and tolerance, to name a few attributes. The Earth School is evolution of consciousness and service to the Divine Plan. People who are so highly vibrationally counterbalance the negativity of the world's human collective.

Society rests on spiritual progress. Realization of the Soul leads to happiness, and without the Soul, the body is of no use. If there is no spiritual progress, then as a result, intolerance, selfishness, sectarianism, bigotry, and narrow-mindedness prevail, causing hatred and disputes among various groups.

If you find yourself thinking of an upsetting or traumatic memory, put on music. Classical, jazz, swing, big band, rock, inspirational—any music that will change your mood and get you out of this record that keeps playing in your head. When listening to the music, you can change the emotional charge of that memory. Then there is the surrendering it over to a higher power, God, Source, the Divine Presence—whatever name you want to identify with is fine. This is where the power is, where you surrender the outcome. Thy Will Be Done, in your life. Be okay with whether you get to go out with your friends or not; either way, there is no complaining.

Source is the treasure of all powers. This power is within us, and when we connect internally, we gain strength. Once this strength is received, the solution to our problems comes to our mind, and we find the courage to bear our adversities. Since our Soul is a piece of Source, it has great strength.

Every Soul has to make their own effort and gain their own experience. Spiritual life proof does not lie in the outer religious buildings, temples, churches, and mosques. Its proof lies in the fact that various individuals have personally experienced and are experiencing this higher inner reality of the Divine within. When this realization is attained, everything else is of no consequence.

A diamond has a brilliance and value. If you toss the diamond into the ground and it is covered with mud, it has not lost its value or shine. You may not see the sheen, yet if you wash it, you will see the original brilliance and value. Similarly, the Soul is a piece of Divine Source, immortal and eternal. When the Soul is placed into a physical form, it has taken on a covering and has lost the appearance of its brilliance and value. Then comes a saint or a mystic who shares how each person's true identity is a Divine Soul. Revealing their true identity removes the coverings of their egoic mind from the Soul, and its brilliance and value are visible. The fortunate people become whole and free because they will be able to see the Divine Presence within themselves.

As you get higher, people won't resonate with you. Everyone is on their own journey. Letting go is cleansing. As some point, you will let people in who resonate with you. What is most important is you being your true, authentic self.

The deepest spiritual path is Self-Realization and God Realization attainment.

Lightworkers, you are the Watchful Guardians of Earth. You came here to be in human form. The Earth is very dense and dark. This is why you came here. Now you see why this is a very important mission for you. Guardians were needed to be among the human collective. When you get overwhelmed by all the dark corruption, remember who you are and why you came here. If you see yourself as broken. You are unbroken and have forgotten your true identity. I am here to remind you, dear Lightworker, that you are in service to the Divine Plan. I know that your heart aches, you hurt, and you miss your home, the dimension from which you came prior to incarnation here on Earth. Stay strong, stay encouraged, and stay on track. Keep moving forward. Your light is needed here. Find a community of other Lightworkers, for this will help you. You will look back and not feel this life was wasted. You will see on the other side after you have translated from this life how much you have helped. You said you wanted to be tested. Lightworker, remember this is really between you and Source.

When you really understand that the Beloved is always with you, remembrance comes.

Do not resist emotions. There are going to be days when you are going to be upset, worried, panicked, and angry, to name a few. You are being human, and emotional responses are normal.

Spiritual progress is earned.

A spiritual path is not straight up the mountain. There are moments when the path is unpredictable. There are times when the path will be intense spiritual passion and devotion. There are times when you will sacrifice everything. At times, you will experience a plateau. A Master Soul Teacher will know that there are times when spiritual growth is so quick that it feels like an avalanche and they are drowning in it, with expansion coming in so fast. Then there are times on the path when they will experience spiritual dryness. You come to a level where you have no dependence on continually seeing and experiencing the spiritual visions because there is this out-there-ness. All the reality is the Oneness, the reality of the Whole. You get to a level where you experience your Divinity Within. Therefore, you are not requiring experience anymore because you know. You eventually come to a level where you have completed all your life lessons, your goals, and your spiritual attainments and you have permission to leave. It comes to a realization that once you reach a high level, you are here on this planet because your frequency is so high and your force benefits life on this planet and the planet itself as well. Whether you leave or go is immaterial, so you might as well stay in physicality and benefit life on this planet since you are already here. You will also find there will be periods of seclusion and living a monastic lifestyle in order to do the inner work required to achieve high spiritual attainments. Then you step out to take on your assignment for service to the Divine Plan.

The opposite of ego is humility.

Spiritual truth attracts people because of its integrity. There is an attraction to the type of person at a higher consciousness level. People at a lower consciousness level would reject truth because their level of truth is based on falsehood; they are not interested in facing the ultimate truth.

When you get to a certain level of consciousness, you start being accountable, taking responsibility, and consciously evolving.

When we have a close friend and are separated from them, we become anxious to be with them again. People who are filled with love for connection with Source are filled with love for the Divine Essence. They have a longing and yearning to go back home. These are the blessed ones.

You become a peacemaker when you are able to obtain peace within yourself. When the Soul gets released from the ego, peace is obtained, and we are able to become Self-Realized. This is when you can live at peace within yourself. Then you are able to radiate peace around yourself and share peace with others. The public may cause you heartache. The human collective is focused on the outward, and your way is inward, so try not to worry how the world treats you. You are in good company, my friend, for many saints, prophets, and Master Soul Teachers were mistreated by the world. You will see this Earth as a dark place. You are the light of the world. Lightworker, don't underestimate your light within yourself. Wherever you go in this world, you will spread this light, peace, and contentment.

Experiencing the separation causes you to seek the union and Oneness with the Divine Presence within yourself.

Your heart has to become pure. Always have a deep, yearning love for the Divine Essence in your heart. Union and Oneness come when your heart is filled with Divine Love.

There is no you. There is only Source. That piece of Source within you is your Soul. See how important you are? Your personal sense of identity is your ego and personality. You are a Divine Being in a physical form having a human experience.

When you are living according to the will of your egoic mind, that is not living at all. When you live by Divine Will, you have no will of your own because you have risen above the realm of the mind and illusion.

The light shines in the darkness. The ego prevents the light of the Soul from shining through. The ego is the covering and the barrier between Soul and Source. When the ego is lowered, then the connection, the Oneness, is experienced. The darkness is an illusion because when the light shines, the darkness disappears. We want to eliminate this veil of darkness and realize the Divine Source within ourselves. It is the Soul within that shines when the darkness is removed. The inner light and sound are from the energy of the Soul.

When you have the Creator, you automatically have the creation.

People can be jealous of you and cause you problems. Pay no attention to them.

When you lower your ego, you are filled with love and humility.

Source is within every one of us. Try to stay positive with negative people. Try to see that it is just their egoic mind that is negative. No matter what negative people say, just respond, "Have a good day!" Stay positive and walk away.

Even if the whole world tries to dissuade you from your path toward Self-Realization and God Realization, you will not leave this journey toward these attainments. That is Faith!

Who are the living dead? Those who have forgotten the Divine. They are living in the world so deeply they have forgotten their true identity as a Divine Being. At some point, these people will hear the Voice of the Divine and become filled with love and service to the Divine Plan.

Your inner experiences are your personal treasure between you and the Divine.

A person who realizes that Source is within their body knows that the highest and greatest is in their human temple.

A diamond never loses its value. The Soul is always shining like the sun.

We are given a number of breaths allotted to us. Make the most use of your allotted breaths.

Love the Creator in the creation.

Soul is a piece of Source.

Enchantment

Divine Love Call
Flows abundantly
Seize a cup
Consume profoundly

Heart is bursting
Overflowing shift
Upward movement
Bliss Delight

Be Consumed
Intimacy of joy
Euphoria Indulgence
Divine Enchantment

Magnetic attraction
Divine Love Call
Whispering captivation
Complete persuasion

—Nancy Clark

Precious One

Who is wiping your tears?
Feeling all your sorrows
Embracing the wisdoms
Caressing the heart

This drama of life
Exciting and Exhausting
Let the Cosmic Wave
Carry you to Love

Shaking of the cage
Notice this reality
Causes the awareness
Seeing more clearly

Behold Ascendance
Precious One
A new chronicle
Higher view perspective

Drink deeply
This fountain
Of Love
Eternally

—Nancy Clark

Beloved's Arrow

Souls ask, "What is Divine Love like?"
You are walking toward Home, and one day the
Beloved's Arrow pierces your heart so deeply.
You cry not because the pain hurts,
you know it is the arrow that caused the Union.
Even though the agony is from the arrow,
you keep this in your heart.
You are so overwhelmed by the arrow, for it is a direct hit.
The Divine precision, a bull's-eye, in the center of the heart.
Divine Love cannot be learned in a book.
You have to experience this arrow.
You can spend a lifetime waiting for the
Beloved's Arrow to come.
When the Divine Presence shoots the arrow,
it never misses the target.
Once pierced, you won't be able to hide this arrow.
You happily serve the Beloved.
Whatever is asked, you place your hand over your heart,
you feel the Beloved's Arrow.
The arrow of Divine Love is Bliss.
You cry because you know how precious this Beloved's Arrow is,
you keep it there as a remembrance.
You ache so deeply.

No one understands this deep anguish of Union
that comes from the arrow.
You will spend the rest of your life trying to explain it.
You know deep down it has to be experienced.
Only then does the Soul know how deep this arrow goes within.
The Beloved's Arrow brings the absorption of Divine Love.
Watch a child when given a new puppy.
The child is so absorbed that it only beholds and desires to be with the puppy.
You walk through this life treasuring the Beloved's Arrow Within.
The Beloved's Arrow of Divine Love causes the metamorphoses.

—Nancy Clark

A Mystical Journey

This Sacred Journey takes place in Four Stages.

The First Stage is called *the Quest*, which causes a calling and search toward spiritual wisdoms and transformation. The heart is pierced by the Divine Presence Within the person, and the spiritual journey begins.

The Second Stage is called *the Surrender*, where the Personal Will is surrendered to the Divine Will for the person's life. This starts a yearning of wanting to have more of their attention focused on a spiritual life and serving the Divine Plan.

The Third Stage is called *the Union*, which causes a mystical experience or an ecstatic state of being in absorption with the Divine Source. The Higher Self (the Soul) steps into the first position and takes control of the person's life. The ego is spiritualized and now serves the Soul and is enraptured by the Divine Love. Within this stage occurs the mystical experience seeing the True Self without the physical form as pure energy, referred to as Self-Realization.

The Fourth Stage is called *the Bliss*, where the person's consciousness is awakened to the reality of their True Identity as Source. The connection with the physical world disappears, and they come to remember that they are Source manifested into human form. This memory is activated, and the person becomes intoxicated in the Love of Infinite Source. Many times, upon arriving back into this physical reality, the person awakens in tears. Within this stage occurs the mystical experience of God Realization.

It is important to take time alone with the Divine Presence and feel this Love along the journey.

—*Nancy Clark*

About the Author

Nancy Clark holds a Ph.D. in Mystical Research offering spiritual evolution. Dr. Nancy Clark is a Mystic and spiritual teacher who helps sincere seekers with the mystical path of God Realization attainment. Dr. Nancy helps Souls gain the wisdoms from questions that seem a mystery. Connect with a Doctorate Level, Mystical Spiritual Teacher.

nancyclarkphd.com

nancyclarkphd.com